CTS Primary Religious Education

Teacher Book 4

Key Stage 2

Sr. Marcellina Cooney, CP
Co-ordinating Editor

The Way, the Truth and the Life series
Religious Education series for 7 to 11 year olds

CATHOLIC TRUTH SOCIETY
PUBLISHERS TO THE HOLY SEE

Teacher Book 4

Nihil obstat: Father Anton Cowan (Censor)
Imprimatur: The Very Rev Alan Hopes, VG, Westminster, 17th July 2002.

The Nihil obstat *and* Imprimatur *are a declaration that the book or pamphlet is considered to be free from doctrinal or moral error. It is not implied that those who have granted the* Nihil obstat *and the* Imprimatur *agree with the contents, opinions or statements expressed.*

© 2002 The Incorporated Catholic Truth Society
Published 2002 by The Incorporated Catholic Truth Society,
40-46 Harleyford Road, London SE11 5AY
Tel: 020 7640 0042 Fax: 020 7640 0046

ISBN: 978 1 86082 167 7 CTS Code: Pr 05

Designed and Produced by: The Catholic Truth Society/Annabel Blatchford.

Printed by: CKN Print Limited.

Front Cover: Jesus the Teacher © Adrian Barclay.

Also available from CTS in *The Way, the Truth and the Life series*

Key Stage 1 supporting syllabus for RE in Catholic schools: ISBN 978 1 86082 289 6 (Order Ref. Pr 12)
Book 1, Big Book: ISBN 978 1 86082 340 4 (Order Ref. Pr 15)
Book 1, Pupil Book: ISBN 978 1 86082 333 6 (Order Ref. Pr 13)
Book 1, Teacher Book: ISBN 978 1 86082 334 3 (Order Ref. Pr 14)
Book 2, Pupil Book: ISBN 978 1 86082 286 5 (Order Ref. Pr 10)
Book 2, Teacher Book: ISBN 1 86082 285 1 (Order Ref. Pr 11)
Key Stage 2 supporting syllabus for RE in Catholic schools: ISBN 978 1 86082 163 4 (Order Ref. Pr 01)
Book 3, Pupil Book: ISBN 978 1 86082 164 6 (Order Ref. Pr 02)
Book 3, Teacher Book: ISBN 978 1 86082 165 3 (Order Ref. Pr 03)
Book 4, Pupil Book: ISBN 978 1 86082 166 0 (Order Ref. Pr 04)
Book 4, Teacher Book: ISBN 1 86082 167 7 (Order Ref. Pr 05)
Book 5, Pupil Book: ISBN 978 1 86082 195 0 (Order Ref. Pr 06)
Book 5, Teacher Book: ISBN 1 86082 196 0 (Order Ref. Pr 07)
Book 6, Pupil Book: ISBN 978 1 86082 200 1 (Order Ref. Pr 08)
Book 6, Teacher Book: ISBN 1 86082 201 0 (Order Ref. Pr 09)
Key Stage 3 supporting syllabus for RE in Catholic schools: ISBN 186082 085 9 (Order Ref. Ed 07)
The Way, Student's Book, Book 1: ISBN 186082 083 2 (Order Ref. Ed 05)
The Way, Teacher's Book, Book 1: ISBN 186082 084 0 (Order Ref. Ed 06)
The Truth, Student's Book, Book 2: ISBN 186082 101 4 (Order Ref. Ed 08)
The Truth, Teacher's Book, Book 2: ISBN 186082 102 2 (Order Ref. Ed 09)
The Truth, Audio CD: (Order Ref. Ed 12)
The Life, Student's Book, Book 3: ISBN: 186082 129 4 (Order Ref. Ed 10)
The Life, Audio CD: (Order Ref. Ed 13)
Exploring the Mass, Student's Book: ISBN 186082 067 0 (Order Ref. Ed 01)
Exploring the Mass, Teacher's Book: ISBN 186082 066 2 (Order Ref. Ed 02)
Exploring the Mass, Video (40 Minutes): (Order Ref. Ed 03)
Exploring the Mass, for Parish Groups and Communities: ISBN 186082 073 5 (Order Ref. Do 659)
A supplementary resource for Teachers, Parents and Students can be found on the website:
http://www.tere.org – developed to support this series.

Teacher Book 4

INTRODUCTION

The teaching of Religious Education to young children is very challenging. It is particularly difficult to convey theological concepts in a stimulating and meaningful way. Consequently, teachers of these age groups need the help and support of good teaching resources in Religious Education.

I am very pleased to welcome and introduce this Teacher Book, which forms part of the Key Stage 2 material - *'The Way, the Truth and the Life series'* - being published by the CTS.

The Syllabus, Pupil and Teacher Books, which make up this series are based on the *Religious Education Curriculum Directory for Catholic Schools* published by the Bishops' Conference in 1996. The Curriculum Directory is based on the content of the *Catechism of the Catholic Church*.

This project is the fruit of hard work and co-operation between a number of teachers across the country. I thank them, and their collaborators, for all their effort.

Monsignor Michael Keegan has been a great source of encouragement to the teachers involved and produced the theological notes for each of the modules in the syllabus. I thank him warmly.

I trust that all who use this Teacher Book 4 and the corresponding Pupil Book 4 will find them a direct, clear help in the important tasks of enabling their pupils to learn about the Catholic faith and to respond to its invitation with growing faith and generosity.

Vincent Nichols

✠ Vincent Nichols
Archbishop of Birmingham

Teacher Book 4

NOTE FOR USERS

The contents of this **Teacher Book** and the companion **Pupil Book 4** are based on the **Key Stage 2 Syllabus**, which is published as a separate document in this series. These resources cover all the essential content of the *Religious Education Curriculum Directory* of the Bishops' Conference of England and Wales (RECD).

The Syllabus incorporates two attainment targets: learning about the Catholic faith (AT1) and learning from the Catholic faith (AT2). These are set out in the form of specific key learning objectives for each module, and listed at the start of each section in both Teacher and Pupil Books. This syllabus can be used as a guide in curriculum planning or as a framework for developing a scheme of work.

In the **Teacher Book**, the key learning objectives are further developed for each module in the form of a **Theological Introduction** to enrich the teacher's understanding of the content they are about to teach. They are based mainly on the *Catechism of the Catholic Church* (CCC). The **Points for Discussion** and **Further Activities**, Suggestions for Prayer and **Photocopiable Worksheets** are all intended to compliment the Pupil Book and provide suggestions for differentiated work.

The section on **Assessment** offers some guidance on different ways of monitoring pupils' progress. The **Level Descriptors** are based on the non-statutory guidance on RE produced by the Qualifications and Curriculum Authority (QCA). These descriptors have been modified so that they apply specifically to the content of the syllabus and Pupil Book 4. The exemplar **Assessment Tasks** based on each module or unit of work are intended as guidance for teachers.

Teachers will want to further enrich the variety of resources with the use of videos, audio CDs, websites and the use of ICT in general. In the **Appendix** "Praying Twice" Clare Watkins shares some very thoughtful insights into using some of our well-known and newer hymns and songs in an original way with young children. Each song is introduced with suggestions for discussion linking the language and the theology used in the song to the work of the units. The connections are expressed in an adult form for teachers to think about: "when we, as teachers, have 'entered the song' we can truly communicate it as prayer and theology for our children".

The inclusion of website addresses does not necessarily mean that everything on them would be appropriate and therefore should be used at the teacher's discretion.

In time, it is hoped to develop our website *www.tere.org* with ongoing updates for teachers, parents and pupils, so that the content of what is being taught in the classroom is readily accessible to all.

ACKNOWLEDGMENTS

Very grateful thanks are expressed to all those who collaborated in preparing this Teacher Book, in particular:

Theological Introductions to the Modules: Mgr Michael Keegan.

Editorial Team: Louise McKenna, Amette Ley, Elizabeth Redmond, Anthony O'Rourke, Laura Lamb, Fergal Martin, Miriam and Marcellina Cooney.

Professional Curriculum Adviser: Margaret Cooling.

Praying Twice, Appendix: Dr Clare Watkins.

Illustrations: *'Joseph's dream'* p.64 © Peter Dennis/Linda Rogers Associates.

Teacher Book 4

CONTENTS

Introduction 3
Note for Users 4
Acknowledgments 4
Overview of Syllabus - Key Stage 2 6
Methodology 7

1. The Bible 8
Key Learning Objectives 8
Theological Introduction 9
Points for Discussion and Further Activities 10

2. Trust in God 14
Key Learning Objectives 14
Theological Introduction 15
Points for Discussion and Further Activities 16

3. Jesus, the Teacher 20
Key Learning Objectives 20
Theological Introduction 21
Points for Discussion and Further Activities 22

4. Jesus, the Saviour 26
Key Learning Objectives 26
Theological Introduction 27
Points for Discussion and Further Activities 28

5. Mission of the Church 32
Key Learning Objectives 32
Theological Introduction 33
Points for Discussion and Further Activities 35

6. Belonging to the Church 38
Key Learning Objectives 38
Theological Introduction 39
Points for Discussion and Further Activities 40

Photocopy Worksheets 43

Assessment and Levels of Achievement 80
Introduction 80
Levels of Achievement 81

Assessment Tasks 83
Guidance on Marking Assessment Tasks 89

Appendix: 'Praying Twice' 91

OVERVIEW OF KEY STAGE 2 SYLLABUS

	Autumn 1	Autumn 2	Spring 1	Spring 2	Summer 1	Summer 2
YEAR 3	3.1 The Christian Family	3.2 Mary, Our Mother	3.3 Called to Change	3.4 Eucharist	3.5 Celebrating Easter & Pentecost	3.6 Being a Christian
YEAR 4	4.1 The Bible	4.2 Trust in God	4.3 Jesus, the Teacher	4.4 Jesus, the Saviour	4.5 Mission of the Church	4.6 Belonging to the Church
YEAR 5	5.1 Gifts from God	5.2 The Commandments	5.3 Inspirational People	5.4 Reconciliation	5.5 Life in the Risen Jesus	5.6 People of Other Faiths
YEAR 6	6.1 The Kingdom of God	6.2 Justice	6.3 Jesus, Son of God	6.4 Jesus, the Bread of Life	6.5 The Work of the Apostles	6.6 Called to Serve

Teacher Book 4

METHODOLOGY

Our starting point in presenting the religious content specified by the *Religious Education Curriculum Directory* (RECD) should be REVELATION. God is always the initiator in the history of our creation and redemption; it is His revealing of himself that makes classroom religious education possible. To begin with Revelation ensures that we respect the revealed nature of Christian faith.

From Revelation we move onto CHURCH; in other words, we consider how Revelation gives life to the Church. The Church is, at one and the same time, the bearer of God's Revelation and the divinely ordered means by which human beings live out their response to Revelation, enlivened by the Holy Spirit who fills the Church.

From here we focus on two aspects of the Church's response to God's Revelation; CELEBRATION - the liturgical and sacramental life of the Church and LIFE IN CHRIST - the moral life and the pursuit of holiness - both enabled and enlivened by the activity and presence of God in the Church.

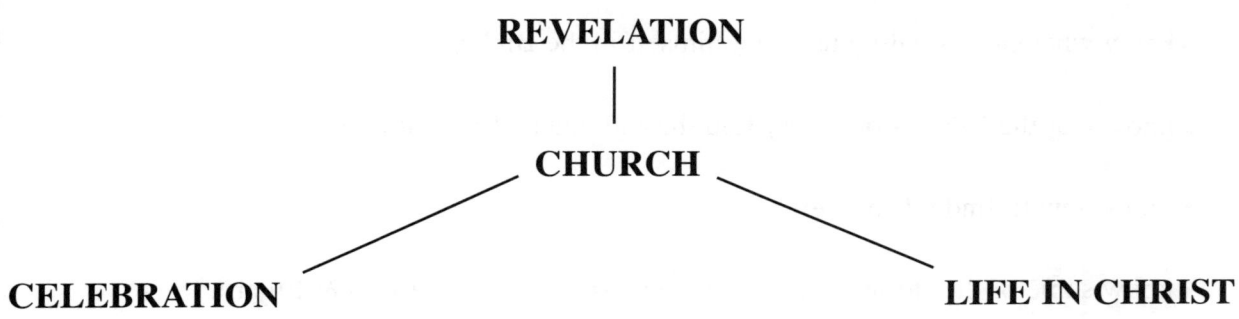

It is proposed that each of these areas should, as far as possible, without artificial distortion of the content areas, be covered in each module of work.

However, attempts to make clear connections between the truths of faith and the pupils' own experience of life are essential. For many it is only when they see the relevance to their own lives of what they are learning that they become fully engaged in it. At times this will mean starting with the pupils' experience. For example, in studying 'conflict and reconciliation' we might well want to begin with reflection on conflict in the lives and experiences of the pupils. Nevertheless, REVELATION in the strict sense of the word would remain the starting point for the delivery and presentation of the specifically religious content material. We would look, in other words, at conflict in our world and in our lives as a sort of background, and then begin our **religious** education proper with how Christian Revelation addresses itself to conflict in human life.

"The Gospel message always, at some point, takes the person beyond the scope of their own experience, challenging and transforming it. It is a message of a saving and transforming gift".
(Archbishop Vincent Nichols)

The Bible

1 THE BIBLE

"The Scriptures are the living Word of God, written under the guidance of the Holy Spirit, received and faithfully handed on within the living Tradition and teaching of the Church." (RECD p.14)

Key learning objectives:

AT 1
In this unit you will have the opportunity to:

- know that the Bible is a story of God's love and concern for us;

- know that the Bible is a living book through which God speaks to us;

- know what God is telling us about himself in the Bible;

- know that the Bible is one story told through many different books;

- know how to find a Bible reference;

- know some of the stories in the Bible (e.g. Moses, David, Jonah & Elijah).

AT 2
You will have the chance to:

- explore how the Bible helps us to pray;

- experience how God speaks to us in the Bible;

- participate in a Bible service;

- experience a guided meditation on a text from the Bible.

The Bible

THEOLOGICAL INTRODUCTION

Q. What is the Bible?

The Bible is also referred to as Sacred Scripture. "All Sacred Scripture is but one book, and this one book is Christ, because all divine Scripture speaks of Christ, and all divine Scripture is fulfilled in Christ" (*CCC 134*). "God is the author of Sacred Scripture because he inspired its human authors; he acts in them and by means of them" (*CCC 136*). "Interpretation of the inspired Scripture must be attentive above all to what God wants to reveal through the sacred authors for our salvation" (*CCC 137*). "The four gospels occupy a central place because Christ Jesus is their centre" (*CCC 139*). "The unity of the two Testaments proceeds from the unity of God's plan and his revelation. The Old Testament prepares for the New and the New Testament fulfils the Old; the two shed light on each other; both are true Word of God" (*CCC 140*). The Bible, therefore, tells us the one story of God's purpose for us, through the many books of which it is made up.

Q. What does God want to reveal through the sacred authors?

"God ...wants to communicate his own divine life to the men he freely created, in order to adopt them as his sons in his only-begotten Son. By revealing himself God wishes to make them capable of responding to him and of knowing him and loving him far beyond their own natural capacity" (*CCC 52*). "...God communicates himself to man gradually. He prepares him to welcome by stages the supernatural Revelation that is to culminate in the person and mission of the incarnate Word, Jesus Christ" (*CCC 53*).

Q. What are the stages in the supernatural Revelation?

1. The Patriarchs. God speaks to Abraham and promises him a people and a place to which to belong and so be secure. The promise matures through Isaac and the people are the twelve tribes, the descendants of the sons of Jacob.

2. Moses. God rescues the people from slavery in Egypt and chooses them to be his own people. He gives them the Holy Law so that they will know how to live at peace with God and with each other. The law also teaches them true worship.

3. The Promised Land. Under Joshua the people enter and settle in Canaan.

4. The Kingdom. The people ask for a king. The promised land becomes a kingdom. David succeeds Saul and, despite serious sin, serves God. His son, king Solomon, builds a great temple in Jerusalem.

5. The Prophets. On the whole, the people were unfaithful and did not keep the Law of God. The first prophets called upon the people to repent and warned of disaster if they failed to repent. The prophets were largely ignored. Disaster came, Jerusalem and the temple were destroyed and the people were taken into exile in Babylon.

6. The Exile. The people in exile, helped by prophets like Ezekiel, edited and ordered their sacred writings. They realised that they had been unfaithful and that they had been warned. They also realised a very profound truth that they were unable to keep God's law by their own strength. They, therefore, looked forward to one who would enable them to live holy lives, a Messiah, One sent by God.

The Bible

7. The Restoration. They were allowed to return to the Holy Land. There the most significant people were the Poor of Yahweh. They wanted a frugal way of life, not because riches were not blessings from God but because riches tempted them to desert God. They lived according to the Law but recognised that they could never be perfect until the Messiah came to save them. They lived for that day.

8. The Messiah. Jesus comes and is welcomed among the Poor of Yahweh. He is Emmanuel and, in him, we are once again made whole and enabled, in him, to live holy lives.

The Bible, therefore, is a story of God's love and concern for us. In the Bible, God is telling us about his plans for our glory and revealing himself to us. The Bible is a living book through which God continually proclaims his call to eternal life.

Q. How can we find a Bible story?
There are 46 books of the Old Testament and 27 books of the New. Each has been given a name. Each is divided into chapters and the verses of each chapter are numbered. To find a Bible story we need to know the name of the book, where it is to be found and the chapter(s) which contain it. It helps to know, also, the verse of the chapter where the story begins.

Q. Where are the stories about Moses, David, Elijah and Jonah in the O. T.?
The stories about Moses begin in the book of Exodus. Chapter 2 and 3 tell of the birth and call of Moses. The book goes on to tell how he brought the Israelites out of Egypt and of the giving of the covenant at Sinai. In chapter 34 of Deuteronomy one can read of his death. The stories about David begin in the first book of Samuel, chapter 16. He features throughout the second book of Samuel and his last days and death are recorded in the first two chapters of the 1st book of Kings. From chapter 17, in the 1st Book of Kings, to chapter 2 in the 2nd Book of Kings are the passages about Elijah. The short Book of Jonah relates the traditions about him.

Q. How does the Bible help us to pray?
"The psalms constitute the masterwork of prayer in the Old Testament. They present two inseparable qualities: the personal and the communal. They extend to all dimensions of history, recalling God's promises already fulfilled and looking for the coming of the Messiah" (*CCC 2596*). "Prayed and fulfilled in the Christ, the psalms are an essential and permanent element of the prayer of the Church. They are suitable for men of every condition and time" (*CCC 2597*). The Bible nourishes faith, hope and charity and teaches us how to live the life of grace.

POINTS FOR DISCUSSION AND FURTHER ACTIVITIES

LEARNING OBJECTIVE: know that the Bible is a story of God's love and concern for us

Discussion points
Throughout the whole Bible there are stories of God's love and concern for us. This topic will come up repeatedly in RE.
- Draw on pupils' experience of what they already know.
- Choose some songs or hymns on the theme, (cf. appendix) and allow the music and words to speak to the pupils.

The Bible

- See if the pupils can recall any stories from the Bible that show God's love and concern.
- Ask them what they think God is really like.
- How do we know what he is like? Make links with the birth of Jesus - who is truly God and truly human, who came down to earth to help us.

LEARNING OBJECTIVE: know that the Bible is a living book through which God speak to us

Discussion points

How do you think God speaks to us through the Bible? St Paul tells us that all scripture can be used to:
- *Teach people,*
- *Correct them when they go wrong,*
- *Guide them in living their lives,*
- *Show them the way to be holy.*

See if pupils can recall examples from what they have already studied to explain what St Paul says, (cf. Book 3 Unit 6 'Being a Christian').

Additional Activities, ICT (Extension)

If pupils have access to computers they might want to open a folder on 'How God speaks to us through the Bible' with files on:
- How God teaches us in the Bible,
- How he corrects people when they go wrong,
- How he is always ready to forgive people who are sorry,
- How he guides us to make the right choices in life,
- How he loves us.

As pupils progress through each unit of their work this year they could keep adding to the files, so that at the end of the year they will have a very clear knowledge and understanding of how God speaks to us in the scriptures.

LEARNING OBJECTIVE: know some of the stories in the Bible

The purpose of these stories is to promote listening skills and give pupils a love for Bible stories.

Moses and the Exodus

If you are reading the story to the pupils invite them to listen out for certain things, for example,
- why Moses went to the King of Egypt,
- how the Israelites were treated in Egypt,
- what type of a man Moses was,
- the description of the different plagues,
- what persuaded Pharaoh to let them go,
- how the Egyptians were stopped from following the Israelites.

The above points could be put on the board before pupils hear the story.

The Bible

Story of David & Goliath

Invite pupils to listen out for certain things in the story, for example,
- what David was like,
- how he fought the giant,
- what people thought would happen to David.

The above points could be put on the board before pupils hear the story.

Drama - Jonah
- See the worksheets for the play on Jonah (p.50). This should help to fire pupils' imagination and draw on their creative talents.
- Before doing this play with the pupils it will help to give them an understanding of who Jonah was and a little bit about the background.
- Jonah was a prophet who lived long ago. A prophet is someone who takes God's messages to the people. One day God asked Jonah to go to the people of Nineveh to tell them that they were behaving badly and God was not pleased with them, they needed to start living good lives or their city would be destroyed.
- Jonah found it very difficult to accept what God was saying to him. The people of Nineveh were the enemy! Why should God want to talk to them? At this time, Jonah did not understand that God cares about everybody - not just the people of Israel. He had to learn that God's love stretches all over the world, he cares about every one of us. He is very reluctant to judge us when we do wrong - but he does want to help us to lead good lives.
- In this story Jonah had to learn that even though he did not want to go to Nineveh, he could not hide from God - not even in the fish! God is everywhere and loves all people.

Further Activity

When the pupils have read the part of the story that is in their books (p.11), ask them to predict what might happen. Did Jonah really go to Nineveh in the end? Did the people repent? Why didn't Jonah want to go?

Extension Activities, The Story of Samuel

Find the story of Samuel's call from God in 1 Samuel 3:1-9. (There are two books called Samuel - you need the first one - 1 Samuel)
  (a) Where was Samuel sleeping?
  (b) Why didn't Samuel know that it was God calling him?
  (c) Whose voice did he think it was?
  (d) What did Eli tell Samuel to say?

Reflection
- Sometimes, we might feel, like Jonah, that we want to try to escape from God, particularly if we think that what God wants us to do is difficult.
- There are other times when we will feel great comfort, because we know that no matter what the difficulties are, God is always with us.
- Let us sit comfortably for a few minutes, close our eyes and just think about the words of this poem from the Bible:

The Bible

> O God, where can I escape from you?
> Where can I be alone?
> If I go up to heaven you are there.
> If I go down to the depths of the earth you are there.
> If I go to the farthest point of the sea,
> Even there your hand guides me.
> Your right hand holds me fast.
> In the darkness of the night
> I am not alone,
> for dark and light are both the same to you.
>
> *(Psalm 139:7-12, adapted)*

Bible Quiz

1. Which part of the Bible comes first?
2. What is the New Testament about?
3. What is the Old Testament about?
4. Name one book from the Old Testament.
5. Name one book from the New Testament.
6. Which book comes before the Gospel of Mark?
7. What books come before the Acts in the New Testament?
8. Name one book with a woman's name in the Old Testament.

ICT Websites

www.calvarychapel.org/children/site/curriculum.htm   OT Stories
www.topmarks.co.uk/judaism/moses/moses1.htm   Moses
www.members.aol.com/bobwhit/bibleWS/jonah.htm   Worksheet on Jonah
www.biblequizzes.com/quest22.htm   Quiz on Jonah
www.members.aol.com/bobwhit/bibleWS/david.htm   Worksheet on David
www.widomaker.com/~flowers/davidgoliath.htm   David
www.ainglkiss.com/bibst/mos1.htm   Moses

Videos

The Story of Moses, The Beginners Bible.
The Story of David and Goliath, The Beginners Bible.
The Story of Jonah and the Whale, The Beginners Bible.

Prayer

God our Father, your word is a light to show me the way to you.
Send your Holy Spirit to help me learn what you want to teach me as I read your word.
I ask this in the name of Jesus Christ. Amen.

Trust in God

2 TRUST IN GOD

"The action of God in the unfolding history of the covenant relationship and the variety of human response is revealed in the Scriptures of the Old and New Testament." (RECD p.14)

Key learning objectives:

AT1
In this unit you will have the opportunity to:

- know Jesus' teaching on the importance of trusting in him;

- know that it is not always easy to trust in God (e.g. Zechariah);

- know the promise God made to Mary through the angel Gabriel;

- know how Joseph put his trust in God when the angel appeared to him;

- be familiar with Mary's song of praise and trust in God, i.e. the Magnificat;

- know that God fulfilled His promise to Mary when Jesus, the Son of God was born.

AT 2
You will have the the chance to:

- deepen our awareness of God's love for us and know that he asks us to trust in Him;

- reflect on times we have found it difficult to trust;

- reflect on the importance of keeping promises;

- make our own Advent promises;

- reflect on how Mary and Joseph placed all their trust in God;

- experience a celebration of the Nativity.

Trust in God

THEOLOGICAL INTRODUCTION

Q. What does Jesus teach about trust in him and trust in God?
"Christ invites us to filial trust in the providence of our heavenly Father cf. Mt 6:26-34,..." (*CCC 322*). Jesus said, "Do not let your hearts be troubled, trust in God still and trust in me" (*John 14:1*).

Q. Is it always easy to trust in God?
"This dramatic situation of 'the whole world [which] is in the power of the evil one' makes man's life a battle: The whole of man's history has been the story of a dour combat with the powers of evil, stretching, so our Lord tells us, from the very dawn of history until the last day. Finding himself in the midst of the battlefield man has to struggle to do what is right, and it is at great cost to himself, and aided by God's grace, that he succeeds in achieving his own inner integrity" (*CCC 409*).

Q. What was the promise made to Mary through the angel Gabriel?
The angel Gabriel said to Mary 'You are to conceive and bear a son and you must name him Jesus. He will be great and will be called Son of the Most High. The Lord will give him the throne of his ancestor David; he will rule over the House of Jacob forever and his reign will have no end.' Mary said to the angel, 'But how can this come about, since I am a virgin?' 'The Holy Spirit will come upon you' the angel answered 'and the power of the Most High will cover you with its shadow. And so the child will be holy and will be called Son of God' (*Luke 1:31-35*).

Q. How did Joseph put his trust in God when the angel appeared to him?
"...the angel of the Lord appeared to him in a dream and said, 'Joseph son of David, do not be afraid to take Mary home as your wife, because she has conceived what is in her by the Holy Spirit. She will give birth to a son and you must name him Jesus, because he is the one who is to save his people from their sins.' ...When Joseph woke up he did what the angel of the Lord had told him to do: he took his wife to his home..." (*Matthew 1:20-25*).

Q. How did Mary trust in God?
"At the announcement that she would give birth to 'the Son of the Most High' without knowing man, by the power of the Holy Spirit, Mary responded with the obedience of faith, certain that 'with God nothing will be impossible': 'Behold, I am the handmaid of the Lord; let it be [done] to me according to your word.'..." (*CCC 494*).

Q. What was Mary's song of praise?
Mary's song of praise is called 'The Magnificat'. It can be found in Luke 1:46-53.

Q. How did God fulfil his promise to Mary?
"So Joseph set out from the town of Nazareth in Galilee and travelled up to Judaea, to the town of David called Bethlehem ...in order to be registered together with Mary, his betrothed, who was with child. While they were there the time came for her to have her child, and she gave birth to a son her first-born" (*Luke 2:4-6*). "The Word was made flesh, he lived among us, and we saw his glory, the glory that is his as the only Son of the Father, full of grace and truth" (*John 1:14*).

Trust in God

Q. How do we know that God loves us?

"Through an utterly free decision, God has revealed himself and given himself to man. This he does by revealing the mystery, his plan of loving goodness, formed from all eternity in Christ, for the benefit of all men. God has fully revealed this plan by sending us his beloved Son, our Lord Jesus Christ, and the Holy Spirit" (*CCC 50*). "By love God has revealed himself and given himself to man" (*CCC 68*). "God, who 'dwells in unapproachable light', wants to communicate his own divine life to the men he freely created, in order to adopt them as his sons in his only-begotten Son..." (*CCC 52*). "A man can have no greater love than to lay down his life for his friends" (*John 15:13*). Our Lord reveals his and the Father's love for us by dying on the cross to redeem us. "With God on our side who can be against us? Since God did not spare his own Son, but gave him up to benefit us all, we may be certain, after such a gift, that he will not refuse anything he can give" (*Romans 8:32*).

Summary

God gradually revealed his purpose for us in the Old Testament. The people of God in the Old Testament were taught to trust that God would send them a saviour of the house of David, a Messiah, filled with the Holy Spirit. God fulfilled the promise, first made to Abraham, when Jesus was born at Bethlehem. In view of all the wonderful works of God, we can joyfully trust that what God has revealed in Christ Jesus, our Lord, he will bring to fulfilment in each one of us, whatever difficulties with which we may meet.

POINTS FOR DISCUSSION AND FURTHER ACTIVITIES

LEARNING OBJECTIVE: know that Jesus teaches us to have faith and trust in him

Discussion

- Focus on questions of meaning and purpose in life.
- Question pupils about what they value most in life and what others value. Are there things we value that money cannot buy?
- Help the pupils to understand the concept of 'trust' with a story e.g. the story of Emma learning to swim (Pupil Book p.18).
- Ask pupils to think of what trusting in God, like Emma at the pool, might mean to them. Perhaps they could think of some similes for trust, e.g. trusting in God is like putting your hand in the hand of someone who knows the way when you are walking in the dark - trusting God is a little like 'holding his hand' as we go through life.

LEARNING OBJECTIVE: know that it is not always easy to trust in God (e.g. Zechariah)

Discussion

- What does it mean to trust? Did Zechariah have any good reasons for trusting? How would you have responded if you were in his situation?
- Encourage all pupils to participate, target questions on individuals who tend to leave it to others to respond.
- We all like to have people we can trust - but how do we know if others feel they can trust us? Are we reliable? Can others depend on us to do what we say?
- Know that there are some questions that are difficult to answer. For example, if we ask him for

something that is really important and he does not give us what we want. Try to explain to pupils that God knows what is best for us - even though we believe what we want at this particular time is best for us - God sees into the future and he will give us whatever it is that is going to make us a better person. Ask pupils to think of examples of how having something that is good in itself, may not be the best thing for us. For example, we may want a new computer and ask God for it - but if we got it we might spend all our time on computer games and neglect much more important things that we should be doing.

LEARNING OBJECTIVE: know the promise God made to Mary through the angel Gabriel

Discussion
- Ask questions that are puzzling and make the pupils think.
- Explain to pupils that Mary said 'yes' to God even though she might have had other plans for her future. Ask them if they thought this would have been easy for her. Why do they think she said 'yes'? Make the point that saying 'yes' to God is not always going to be easy.
- Do we say 'yes' to others when it suits us? Can we think of the most recent example when we said 'yes' to someone because we knew it was the right thing to do - even though it was a bit difficult - tidy up after a meal at home when we would have preferred to watch TV - play with a younger brother or sister when we would have preferred to go out with a friend.

Additional Activities
- In groups plan a role-play situation where we are faced with different choices, but we spend a little time thinking of how Jesus would want us to behave before we make a choice - e.g. a group that usually get into trouble invite you to go out with them; or the teacher has to leave the room for a few minutes - do you take advantage of the situation to stop working or cause trouble?
- Each group does the role-play for the rest of the class - but 'freeze' it just before the end to give the class time to discuss the dilemma, then allow the group to show how they made the right decision. Afterwards ask them why they made that decision.
- Pupils could make their own angels for their Christmas tree. They could use different shaped bases, e.g. triangular, rectangular etc for the body, add wings, head etc.

Prayer
God our Father,
Mary our Mother was always ready to do whatever you asked of her.
Help us to be more like Mary so that we are ready to listen to your voice.
Help us to be willing to do what you ask of us.
Give us the help we need to show kindness to those we meet.

LEARNING OBJECTIVE: know that God fulfilled his promise to Mary when Jesus was born

Discussion
- Ask the pupils why they think that it was part of God's plan to have Jesus born in a stable. What if Jesus had been born in a palace as part of a powerful family - then he could have made sure everyone followed his teachings. Why did God choose to send his Son into a poor family?

Trust in God

- Why do the pupils think that the shepherds were the first to be invited to see the Son of God?

Additional Activities
- Think of some promises you could make to God during Advent.
- Write your Advent promises in a list. Roll up your paper to make a scroll and keep it in a safe place where you can look at it often.
- Have a large collection of Christmas cards spread out on a table, the majority with a religious significance, but some with just secular greetings. Invite the pupils to study them for a few moments and then to choose the one that they like the most. If two or three want the same card let them sit together. When they have had some time to reflect on why they chose a particular card invite them to make a quick sketch of the picture on the card and then underneath it to write down what they like about it and why they chose it.
- The pupils could use some of the ideas on these Christmas cards to make a card for their family or friends.
- Research: What was the news that the angel brought to the shepherds? How would they know it had come true? Clue Luke 2:9-12.
- Make a picture of the Nativity scene which emphasises the importance of the child Jesus in some way, e.g, the figure is larger in proportion, in colour while the rest is in black and white, textured, all the figures face the child, the child is 3D...

ICT
www.topmarks.co.uk/christianity/nativity/nativity1.htm   Mary and the Angel; Journey to Bethlehem; No Room in the Inn
www.catholic.org/saints   Saints
www.cptryon.org/prayer/child/adv.html   Advent wreath and prayers for each week
www.ainglkiss.com/saints/gabr.htm   St Gabriel
www.calvarychapel.org/children/site/curriculum_n.htm   NT stories e.g. Zechariah & Elizabeth; Gabriel visits Mary; the birth of Jesus; Angels appear to shepherds; Escape to Egypt
www.ewtn.com/Gallery/tnt/nt2s.htm   The Flight into Egypt

Videos
Mary & Joseph, Saints for Kids, Vol 1, St Paul's Multimedia.
Elizabeth and Zechariah, Saints for Kids, Vol 2.

Trust in God

Guided Meditation, Trusting in God

Invite the pupils to make themselves comfortable, to sit back on their chair with both feet flat on the ground. Invite them to close their eyes and just to trust in Jesus.

Imagine we are going out into a beautiful place in the country. The sky is blue and the sun is shining. We go into a field where there are lots of wild flowers, bluebells, primroses, daisies and dandelions. The birds are singing in the trees, we can see a blackbird making a nest on one of the branches. Below there is a stream with a duck and tiny ducklings swimming merrily around.

Most of all, we want to sit still and think of what Jesus teaches us about the birds in the air and the flowers in the field. We listen to his words very carefully:
Jesus asks us to really trust in him. This is what he says:

Look at the birds in the sky. They do not sow or reap or gather into barns; yet your heavenly Father feeds them. Are you not worth much more than they are? Can any of you imagine just how much I care about you?

Think of the flowers growing in the fields; they never have to work or spin yet God looks after them. Now if that is how God clothes the wild flowers growing in the fields, how much more will he look after you, if you have faith and trust in him. (Matthew 6:28-30, adapted).

Now, take a few deep breaths and send away all your worries and concerns. Just let your body become loose and relaxed.

Jesus tells us not to worry. Think of the things that worry you. [Pause]

Let us ask Jesus to take our worries from us. [Pause]

Now let us thank God in our hearts for all the wonderful things he has given to us, eyes to be able to see the beauty of creation, ears to hear the birds singing and wonderful voices to be able to sing and thank God for his goodness to us.

Hymn of praise and thanksgiving e.g. 'All creation bless the Lord' (HON 9).

Jesus, the Teacher

3 JESUS, THE TEACHER

"God's Self-Revelation and the covenant relationship reach their fullness in Jesus Christ, the only-begotten Son of God. He is truly God and, as a man, truly human. His life, death and resurrection are the central event of all human history and at the heart of faith. His cross is the sign of his unique offering of himself for each and every human being. As truly God, Jesus reveals the truth and love of God; as truly human, Jesus reveals the perfect response to God and intimate communion with his Father - 'Abba'." (RECD p.14)

Key learning objectives:

AT 1
In this unit you will have the opportunity to:

- know that Jesus was born a Jew;

- know the story of the presentation of Jesus in the Temple;

- know that Jesus attended synagogue as a child and as an adult and read the Torah;

- know that Jesus travelled around teaching people about God and His kingdom;

- understand why Jesus used parables to teach people;

- know and understand some of the parables Jesus told.

AT 2
You will have the chance to:

- appreciate the relevance of the parables for us today;

- recognise that Lent is an opportunity for us to change our behaviour and live as Jesus told us.

Jesus, the Teacher

THEOLOGICAL INTRODUCTION

Q. To what people did Jesus belong?
"We believe that Jesus of Nazareth, born a Jew of a daughter of Israel..." (*CCC 423*). "Many Jews and even certain Gentiles who shared their hope recognised in Jesus the fundamental attributes of the messianic 'Son of David', promised by God to Israel" (*CCC 439*). Jesus was a descendant of Abraham of the line of king David.

Q. Why was Jesus presented in the Temple? What happened at the presentation?
"*The presentation of Jesus in the temple* shows him to be the firstborn Son who belongs to the Lord. With Simeon and Anna, all Israel awaits its encounter with the Saviour... Jesus is recognised as the long-expected Messiah, the 'light of the nations' and the 'glory of Israel', but also a 'sign that is spoken against'. The sword of sorrow predicted for Mary announces Christ's perfect and unique oblation on the cross that will impart the salvation God had 'prepared in the presence of all peoples'" (*CCC 529*). For what happened at the Presentation see St Luke 2:22-40.

Q. How did Jesus keep the Sabbath day?
"He came to Nazara, where he had been brought up and went into the synagogue on the Sabbath day as he usually did. He stood up to read, and they handed him the scroll of the prophet Isaiah" (*Luke 4:16-17*). Our Lord attended the synagogue as a child with Mary and Joseph. There he was taught the scriptures and worshiped with the people of Nazareth. All his life he kept the law and observed the Sabbath by worshiping in the synagogue and in the Temple at Jerusalem.

Q. How did Jesus proclaim his message?
"He went round the whole of Galilee teaching in their synagogues, proclaiming the Good News of the kingdom..." (*Matthew 4:23*). "Now after John was arrested, Jesus came into Galilee, preaching the gospel of God, and saying: 'The time is fulfilled, and the kingdom of God is at hand: repent and believe in the gospel. To carry out the will of the Father, Christ inaugurated the kingdom of God on earth.' Now the Father's will is 'to raise up men to share in his own divine life'. He does this by gathering men around his Son Jesus Christ. This gathering is the Church, 'on earth the seed and beginning of the kingdom'" (*CCC 541*). Our Lord also preached in Judaea and especially in Jerusalem. He preached to the Samaritans (*John 4*). Our Lord also taught by what he did. His death on the cross teaches us how much the Father loves us for he gave us his only Son. It shows us how much Jesus loves us for he was willing to give his life to destroy our sins. His resurrection reveals the eternal life which he offers to all who will believe in him.

Q. Why did Jesus teach in parables?
"Jesus' invitation to enter his kingdom comes in the form of *parables*, a characteristic feature of his teaching. Through his parables he invites people to the feast of the kingdom, but he also asks for radical choice: to gain the kingdom, one must give everything. Words are not enough, deeds are required. The parables are like mirrors for man: will he be hard soil or good earth for the word? What use has he made of the talents he has received? Jesus and the presence of the kingdom in this world are secretly at the heart of the parables. One must enter the kingdom, that is become a disciple of Christ, in order to 'know the secrets of the kingdom of heaven'. For those who stay 'outside', everything remains enigmatic" (*CCC 541*). When asked by the disciples "Why do you talk to them in parables?" Jesus replied... "the reason I talk to them in parables is that they look without seeing and listen without hearing or understanding" (*Matthew 13:10,14,34,35; Luke 8:9-10*).

Jesus, the Teacher

Q. What were some of the parables, which Jesus used?

To teach that words are not enough, see the parable of the two sons, Matthew 22:28-32. Hard soil or good earth for receiving the word of God? See Matthew 13; Mark 4; Luke 8. To understand who is our neighbour, see The Good Samaritan in Luke 10. To hear about God's mercy for the sinner, see the parable of the lost sheep, the parable of the prodigal son, and the parable of the tax collector and the Pharisee (*Luke chapters 15 and 18*). The parables strike into our hearts today just as they did then. They present us with radical choices. Our Lord was a brilliant teacher!

Q. What does the Church call us to do during Lent?

On Ash Wednesday we are exhorted to turn away from sin and to be faithful to the gospel. We are asked to make the season of Lent holy by self-denial and works of charity. We pray in the third preface of Lent, 'You ask us to express our thanks by self-denial. We are to master our sinfulness and counter our pride. We are to show those in need your goodness to ourselves.' The season of Lent is a preparation for the celebration of Easter. The liturgy prepares the catechumens for the celebration of the paschal mystery by the several stages of Christian initiation: it also prepares the faithful who recall their baptism and do penance in preparation for Easter (*See Roman Missal - General norms 27*). At Easter all renew their baptismal promises.

Summary

Jesus himself is our example. All his teachings show how deeply he had studied the Old Testament. He used the teachings of the Old Testament to show how he himself was the fulfilment of those teachings. In himself he revealed what the Old Testament could only hint at because his revelation transcended the expectations aroused under the old covenant. The glory of his life, death, resurrection and ascension into glory totally surpass even the greatest of God's deeds in the history of Israel.

POINTS FOR DISCUSSION AND FURTHER ACTIVITIES

Information

The Bible speaks of God's people in several ways. Sometimes they are called **The Hebrews** after Abraham. The Bible speaks of him as "Abram the Hebrew" in Gen 14:3. (This was before God changed his name to Abraham.) Hebrew is also the name of the language the people spoke.

Sometimes God's people are called **Israelites**, or the children of Israel. Israel was the new name God gave to Jacob, the son of Isaac, the son of Abraham (Gen 32:27-28). Sometimes God's people are called **Jews**. This sounds like 'Judah', which was the name of one of Jacob's twelve sons.

> **LEARNING OBJECTIVE: know the story of the Presentation of Jesus in the Temple**

Information

The Feast of 'The Presentation of Jesus in the Temple' is on 2nd February each year. Sometimes there is a procession with lighted candles at Mass on this day, so it is also called 'Candlemas'. The significance of the lighted candles is that Jesus is the 'light' that has come into the world.

Jesus, the Teacher

Discussion
Why do the pupils think Simeon was so happy to see the infant Jesus? How did he know who Jesus was? What do they think he meant by saying "my eyes have seen your salvation"? Who is the Messiah? (*Explain that Messiah is another name for 'saviour' and that Jesus had come to save all people. It literally means 'Anointed One'*).

Activities
- On a globe or in an atlas, find some of the countries where there is war or famine at the moment.
  (a) Write the names of these countries on a card for display.
  (b) In groups, choose one of these countries and write a prayer to Jesus 'light of the world' for it.
  (c) Arrange a little prayer service for all the countries where there is war or famine. If possible, light a candle for each country.
- Write out these promises God made to the Jewish people and put them with the correct people.

David   God promised he would be the father of a great nation. (*Gen 22:17*)

Moses   God showed him a ladder reaching to heaven and promised to bring him back to his country and give him many descendants. (*Gen 28:15*)

Abraham   God promised that his house and his kingdom would last forever. (*II Sam 16-17*)

Jacob   God promised he would bring his people out of Egypt into the land he promised Abraham. (*Ex 6:7-8*)

Prayer
This Prayer of Simeon is used at the end of every day in the Prayer of the Church.

> "Lord, now let your servant depart in peace according to your word,
> for my eyes have seen your salvation
> which you have prepared in the sight of all the peoples,
> a light for the nations and the glory of your people Israel." (*Luke 2:29-32*)

LEARNING OBJECTIVE: Know that Jesus travelled around teaching people

Information

The Temple
There was only one Temple and it was in Jerusalem.
The Temple was the house of God where Jews believed that God was present in the Ark of the Covenant.
The Jews went to the Temple to worship God and offer sacrifices.

The Synagogue
There was a synagogue in every Jewish town.
The synagogue is a meeting place.
The Jews go to the Synagogue to meet together to pray, to learn the Holy Scriptures, and to help each other.

The Torah
The name for the first five books of the Bible; these books are also know as the Law or Pentateuch. They are especially sacred to the Jews.

Jesus, the Teacher

Discussion

- It must have felt strange to Jesus to come back to his hometown and teach in the synagogue where he had been as a child. Ask the pupils to imagine they are grown up and coming back to their school as a teacher. How would they feel? What do they think the older teachers would think of them - the ones who used to be their teachers? Would they be worried that they would not be taken seriously?
- It was hard for the people to understand who Jesus was. They liked to see the sick people made well. They knew they should look after each other. Sometimes Jesus said things they found really hard to understand. Sometimes he forgave somebody their sins and the people knew that only God could forgive sins (*Matt 9:2*). See if the pupils can think of any other reasons why Jesus was not popular with everyone? What did he tell them to do about their enemies? (*Love your enemies, do good to those who hate you... Matt 5:44*).

Activities

- Read how Jesus reminded the people of Nazareth that prophets often have to work in other places because their own people do not have enough faith in them, and what the people did because they were angry (*Luke 4:14-30*). Imagine you were one of the people in the synagogue that day when Jesus was teaching there. Write down your thoughts before he began to speak, and then what you thought at the end, when Jesus was put out of the Synagogue.

LEARNING OBJECTIVE: know that Jesus came to show us the way to live

Discussion

- Discuss with the children the ways in which they are used to helping others, for example, being kind, helping at home, looking after family members, etc. Then tell the parable of the 'Talents' (*Matt 25:15-46*), consider all the talents they have among them, the ability to sing, dance, draw, etc. Ask the pupils to think how they might become involved in fund-raising in order to feed the hungry, etc.
- Jesus asks us to do this: "*Love your enemies and pray for those who persecute you*" (*Matt 5:44*). How easy do the pupils think it is to do this? Can they think of any times when it might be really difficult to pray for their enemies? How can they find help to do this?
- Gospel means 'good news' - we have looked at many things that Jesus has taught us. Invite pupils to be 'Good News' people to all we meet. We can do this by being kind and thoughtful. We can make people feel good about themselves by saying nice things about them. Make a list of some of the things that make us feel good. Think of how we can be 'Good News' people at home and in school.

Activities

- Make a Bible bookmark that will help you to remember one of the important things Jesus has asked us to do, for example, 'be always ready to forgive'.

ICT

- Invite pupils to choose one of the 'sayings' of Jesus that they believe to be very important. See worksheet: 'Know the teachings of Jesus' (p.67) for some useful references. Using ICT skills the pupils could make a large poster of these words, decorate them and use them for display work in the classroom. They could also serve as a reminder of how we ought to behave and to treat each other.

Jesus, the Teacher

LEARNING OBJECTIVE: know that Jesus used parables to teach people

Parables are stories told by Jesus to communicate a religious truth. Often they have just one main point. There is an opportunity here to recap on the parables covered in Pupil Book 3: 'The Lost Sheep' page 36; 'The Lost Son' page 40; 'The Good Samaritan', Teacher Book 3 page 76.

The parable of **'The Sower'** (*Luke 8:4-15*)
This parable help pupils to understand that we can all be like the different types of seed. There are times when we may forget the Word of God and can be selfish or unkind, and there are times when we are very generous and helpful towards other people.

Activities

- In the parable of 'The Great Feast', (p.68) invite the children to write an alternative ending - suppose the guests had not made excuses.
- Can we think of anything today that Jesus invites us to celebrate? How do we respond?
- Invite the pupils to choose their favourite parable to prepare a role-play for the class.
- Design a wall poster to illustrate your favourite parable. Make sure the main characters are bold and clear and that the message is obvious. Here are some to choose from with references to help you, or you can use one you already know.

The Mustard Seed	Matt 13:31,32 Mark 4:30-32 Luke 13:18,19
The Rich Fool	Luke 12:16-21
The Travelling Owner of the House	Mark 13:34-37
The Lost Coin	Matt 15:8-10

ICT

www.jesusisajew.org/Jesus_is_a_Jew.htm   For teachers - short, clear page on Jesus as a Jew.
www.angelfire.com/zine/childrenhelping/   For teachers - information on various fundraising projects to raise awareness. Most children will be able to read about the projects for themselves here.
www.ainglkiss.com/stories/gb2.htm   God's Book, New Testament, very useful to help pupils recap on how to look up a reference.
www.ainglkiss.com/teaches/   What Jesus teaches us

Jesus, the Saviour

4 JESUS, THE SAVIOUR

"[Jesus'] life, death and resurrection are the central event of all human history and at the heart of faith. His cross is the sign of his unique offering of himself for each and every human being." (RECD p.14)

Key learning objectives:

AT 1
In this unit you will have the opportunity to:

- know that Jesus came to share our life so that we can share his life;
- know that Jesus is truly God and, as man, truly human;
- know that Jesus came to show us the way to live;
- know that when Jesus died on the cross he took away our sins;
- know what happened in Holy Week;
- know what happened on Easter Sunday.

AT 2
You will have the chance to:

- reflect on how we can share in the life of Jesus;
- appreciate that Jesus is truly God and, as man, truly human;
- take part in some of the Holy Week services;
- reflect on the importance of the Resurrection for us.

Jesus, the Saviour

THEOLOGICAL INTRODUCTION

Q. How did Jesus come to share our human life?
"...the Son of God assumed a human nature in order to accomplish our salvation in it..." (*CCC 461*). "Because the human nature was assumed, not absorbed, in the mysterious union of the Incarnation, the Church was led over the course of centuries to confess the full reality of Christ's human soul, with the operations of intellect and will, and of his human body. In parallel fashion, she had to recall on each occasion that Christ's human nature belongs, as his own, to the divine person of the Son of God, who assumed it. Everything that Christ is and does in this nature derives from 'one of the Trinity'. The Son of God therefore communicates to his humanity his own personal mode of existence in the Trinity. In his soul as in his body, Christ thus expresses humanly the divine ways of the Trinity.

The Son of God... worked with human hands; he thought with a human mind. He acted with a human will, and with a human heart he loved. Born of the Virgin Mary, he has truly been made one of us, like to us in all things except sin" (*CCC 470*).

Q. How do we share in the life of Jesus?
"The Word became flesh to make us *'partakers of the divine nature'*: For this is why the Son of God became the Son of man: so that man, by entering into communion with the Word and thus receiving divine sonship, might become a son of God.' 'For the Son of God became man so that we might become God.' 'The only-begotten Son of God, wanting to make us sharers in his divinity, assumed our nature, so that he, made man, might make us gods" (*CCC 460*). "...Jesus spoke of a still more intimate communion between him and those who would follow him: 'Abide in me and I in you... I am the vine and you are the branches.' And he proclaimed a mysterious and real communion between his own body and ours: 'He who eats my flesh and drinks my blood abides in me, and I in him" (*CCC 787*).

Q. How did Jesus reveal that he was truly God?
"Jesus gave scandal above all when he identified his merciful conduct towards sinners with God's own attitude towards them. He went so far as to hint that by sharing the table of sinners he was admitting them to the messianic banquet. But it was most especially by forgiving sins that Jesus placed the religious authorities of Israel on the horns of a dilemma. Were they not entitled to demand in consternation, 'Who can forgive sins but God alone?' By forgiving sins Jesus either is blaspheming as a man who made himself God's equal, or is speaking the truth and his person really does make present and reveal God's name" (*CCC 589*). "Only the divine identity of Jesus' person can justify such a claim as 'He who is not with me is against me'; and his saying that there was in him 'something greater than Jonah,... greater than Solomon', something 'greater than the Temple'; his reminder that David called the Messiah his Lord, and his affirmations, 'Before Abraham was, I Am', and even 'I and the Father are one'" (*CCC 590*). His claim to be Son of God is vindicated in his resurrection.

Q. What did Jesus teach us about the way to live?
"In all his life Jesus presents himself as *our model*. He is 'the perfect man', who invites us to become his disciples and follow him. In humbling himself, he has given us an example to imitate, through his prayer he draws us to pray, and by his poverty he calls us to accept freely the privation and persecutions that may come our way" (*CCC 520*).

Jesus, the Saviour

Q. What did Jesus' death on the cross accomplish?

"Christ's death is both the *Paschal sacrifice* that accomplishes the definitive redemption of men, through 'the Lamb of God who takes away the sins of the world', and the *sacrifice of the New Covenant*, which restores man to communion with God by reconciling him to God through the 'blood of the covenant, which was poured out for many for the forgiveness of sins'" (*CCC 613*).

Q. What happened in Holy Week?

Holy Week begins with the entry of our Lord into Jerusalem, riding on a colt, while the people shouted '*Hosanna! Blessings on him who comes in the name of the Lord!*' Many spread their cloaks on the road, others greenery which they had cut in the fields. On the Thursday the Lord celebrated the Passover supper with his apostles. At this last supper, our Lord changed bread and wine into his body and blood. He commanded the apostles to do the same as a memorial of his passion and death until he comes. Then he went to the garden of Gethsemane where he suffered great agony of mind. He prayed to his Father to let the cup of suffering pass him by but he accepted his Father's will. In the garden Judas Iscariot betrayed him to those who came from the chief priests to arrest him. They condemned him to death. On the Friday morning they accused him before Pilate who tried to release him but he gave way to them and condemned him to crucifixion. He was scourged and crowned with thorns and carried his cross to the place of execution. On the way the soldiers compelled Simon from Cyrene to help carry the cross. He was crucified and died. He was buried in a cave tomb close to Calvary. All the gospels have an account of these events. St Luke adds an account of Pilate sending Jesus to king Herod.

Q. What happened on Easter Sunday?

On Easter Sunday Christ rose from the dead. "...The resurrection of Jesus is the crowning truth of our faith in Christ, a faith believed and lived as the central truth by the first Christian community; handed on as a fundamental by Tradition; established by the documents of the New Testament; and preached as an essential part of the Paschal mystery along with the cross;..." (*CCC 638*). "The mystery of Christ's resurrection is a real event, with manifestations which were historically verified, as the New Testament bears witness..." (*CCC 639*). "By means of touch and the sharing of a meal, the risen Jesus establishes direct contact with his disciples. He invites them in this way to recognise that he is not a ghost and above all to verify that the risen body in which he appears to them is the same body that had been tortured and crucified, for it still bears the traces of his Passion. Yet at the same time this authentic, real body possess the new properties of a glorious body: not limited by space and time but able to be present how and when he wills..." (*CCC 645*).

POINTS FOR DISCUSSION AND FURTHER ACTIVITIES

LEARNING OBJECTIVE: know that Jesus is truly God and, as man, truly human

Discussion
- Remind the pupils of the story of how Jesus was found in the Temple when he was twelve years old, asking questions of the teachers there (*Luke 2:41-51*). What do the children think he was asking the teachers?
- St Luke tells us that Jesus was also giving answers. What question would the children most like to ask Jesus?
- By staying behind in the Temple, Jesus greatly upset his parents. Invite the children to think how their parents might react if they did such a thing.

Jesus, the Saviour

- Why do the children think Jesus said, *"It is easier for a camel to pass through the eye of a needle than for a rich man to enter the kingdom of God"* (*Luke 18:29*). Why might it be very hard for a rich person to be a friend of God?

LEARNING OBJECTIVE: know that Jesus came to share our life so that we can share his life

Discussion
- Ask the pupils if there was a time when they really badly wanted something, perhaps a toy or a treat. Did they get what they wanted? Did it make them happy? Did it make them so happy that they never wanted another toy or treat again?
- Discuss with pupils what true happiness is and how to find it. (*Being at peace with ourselves, with others, with God; telling the truth, being upright and honest etc.*)

Activities
- Sharing in the life of Jesus - Jesus said:
  > "If anyone loves me he will keep my word,
  > and my Father will love him,
  > and we shall come to him
  > and make our home with him." (*John 14:23*)

Invite pupils to tell you what 'words' Jesus will want us to keep, e.g. 'Love one another'. Refer back to an earlier section in the Pupil Book, '*Jesus came to show us the way to live*' (p.38) Pupils should then be able to answer question 1 (a) on page 39 of the Pupil Book.

- Jesus offers us the gift of sharing his life. We are especially close to him at Mass and particularly when we receive him in Holy Communion. At the end of Mass the priest says these or some similar words, "Go in peace to love and serve the Lord."
  (a) Write our response (answer) to this.
  (b) Look at these ways we can 'go in peace' when Mass is over.
  > Light a candle and say a prayer for someone;
  > Help put away the books in the Church
  > Genuflect to Jesus before you leave the Church;
  > Wait until you get outside to start talking and laughing;
  > Do something kind for someone in your family.

  (c) Choose one or two of these ways and draw a picture of yourself doing them.
  (d) Write the words 'Go in Peace' underneath.
- Think about what true happiness is. Write a letter to an imaginary friend explaining what true happiness is and how you can find it.

LEARNING OBJECTIVE: know the events of Holy Week

Palm Sunday: many people were expecting Jesus to ride into the city as a conquering king - not on a donkey! They believed he was a special king whom God had promised to send to them. When they saw him coming they shouted *"Hosanna! Blessings on him who comes in the name of the Lord!"*

Jesus, the Saviour

Holy Thursday: the night before he died Jesus wanted to share a Passover meal with his disciples. It was here that Jesus shared the bread and wine with his disciples telling them it was his Body and Blood. Just as he told us to, we re-present this everyday in the Mass.

Passover: when the Jews celebrate the Passover they recall their escape from slavery in Egypt. The Jews now celebrate the Passover at the 'Pesach' every spring.

Good Friday - Easter Sunday: Jesus died on the Cross and rose from the dead so that we could receive the Spirit - the very life and love of God.

The Resurrection: God accepted Jesus' sacrifice on behalf of us all. Through the Holy Spirit, Jesus is now transformed - no longer subject to death and the effects of sin. He is a new creation; he is Lord!

Discussion
- Good Friday: invite pupils to talk about things that make us sad.
- Peter knew he let Jesus down badly, but the wonderful thing he discovered was that Jesus did not hold it against him. Jesus forgave him and later made him the leader of the Apostles. Encourage the pupils to share experiences of forgiving others and being forgiven and how this helps to build stronger relationships.
- On Good Friday Jesus' friends felt that everything had gone terribly wrong for them. Their hopes and expectations were shattered. They had believed that Jesus was God's special king, but it looked as if they had been mistaken. It is important not to dwell on the events of Good Friday - it was not the end of the story. It is a sad day - it shows us that Jesus was prepared to give his life for us because of his love for us. Show how he was prepared to forgive the repentant thief on the cross.
- Are there occasions when we feel shattered? What can we learn from the experience of the disciples?
- For us, the cross is a symbol of victory, through it Jesus conquered death and overcame wrongdoing. Love conquered hatred and life overcame death. Jesus broke the power of evil in the world; even though we still have to conquer selfishness, jealousy and other tendencies towards wrongdoing, we know that Jesus is always ready to forgive us, and to help us in our daily lives. What is the sacrament we can receive each time we want to tell Jesus we are sorry for our wrongdoing and ask for his help to lead a good life? This can be an opportunity to recap on the Sacrament of Reconciliation.
- The Resurrection: Jesus rose from the dead and showed that death is not the end for him. He has come to share eternal life with us. Jesus said, "I am the Resurrection and the Life. Whoever believes in me will live, even though he/she dies." (*John 11:25*) Explain to pupils that we believe by faith that Jesus rose from the dead. Invite pupils to grapple with the mystery of the Resurrection. Ask questions such as: Why do you think the disciples didn't know that Jesus would rise from the dead? Why do you think Mary Magdalene did not recognise Jesus straight away? What about the disciples on the road to Emmaus? What would happen if...? Does anyone else have a different idea?

Activities
- Read again the account of Peter in the courtyard saying that he did not know Jesus. Draw a picture of Peter immediately after the cock crew and in a big thought bubble write some of the thoughts you think were going on in his head.

Jesus, the Saviour

- When Jesus was on the cross, one of the thieves who was being crucified with him said, "Lord, remember me when you come into your kingdom." Look up Luke 23:43 and write down the reply Jesus gave to him.

LEARNING OBJECTIVE: know what happened on Easter Sunday

Discussion
- Discuss with the children why Easter is such an important feast - more important than Christmas even. Why do the children think that more fuss and bigger celebrations take place (outside of the Church) at Christmas rather than Easter?
- Do the children know about any of the important Easter services in Church? Have any of them ever been taken to the Easter Vigil and seen the New Fire and the new Paschal Candle lit?

Activities
- Imagine you have a chance to interview Mary Magdalene or Thomas after the Resurrection of Jesus. Make a list of the questions you would like to ask them. Now try to answer the questions.
- Using ICT skills design a poster to remind others that Jesus rose from the dead and what that means for us.
- Using ICT skills design a booklet for Year 2 pupils to explain the Easter Story.
- Look at these words which the priest says as he prepares the Paschal Candle:

> Christ yesterday and today,
> the beginning and the end,
> Alpha and Omega,
> all time belongs to him
> and all the ages,
> to him be glory and power
> through every age forever, Amen.

(a) Draw a candle shape and choose one of these lines to write inside it.
(b) Explain why you chose this line.
(c) See if you can find out how to write the Greek letters 'Alpha' and 'Omega' - these are the first and last letters of the Greek alphabet and we always see them on the Paschal Candle.
(d) Have you seen these letters anywhere else in Church?
(e) Can you find out what else is on the Paschal Candle?

ICT Links
www.cptryon.org/prayer/child/lent/holywk/01.html   Excellent for each day of Holy Week & Easter
www.topmarks.co.uk/christianity/easter/easter.htm   The Easter Story
www.catholic-church.org/kuwait/easter_candle.htm   This gives an explanation of the Paschal Candle - accessible to fairly good readers. The renewal of Baptismal Promises is also given.

Mission of the Church

5 Mission of the Church

"Christ inaugurated the Church when he began to proclaim Good News and through the Church he fulfils and reveals God's plan to unite all things in him. Christ gave his Church a structure in calling and choosing twelve apostles. With them and their successors he shares his mission, his power and authority. In the coming of the Holy Spirit at Pentecost the Church was revealed and its mission (apostolate) to the nations was begun... The Church's mission is that of Christ its head. The ultimate purpose of this mission is to enable all people to share in the communion of life and love of the Father, Son and Holy Spirit." (RECD p.19)

Key learning objectives:

AT 1
In this unit you will have the opportunity to:

- know the good news that God the Father sent his Son to save us;

- know that Peter was chosen by Jesus to play a special role in the Church;

- know that Jesus gave his followers a mission - to spread the Good News to others;

- know that Jesus sent his Spirit to help them at Pentecost;

- understand that this was the beginning of the Church;

- know how Saints Peter and Stephen helped to spread the Good News by their lives and their deaths;

- know the story of the coming of the Holy Spirit at Pentecost;

- understand how the coming of the Holy Spirit at Pentecost changed the disciples.

AT 2
You will have the chance to:

- appreciate that we too have a role to play in spreading the Good News;

- identify ways we can spread the Good News in our lives;

- consider ways in which we can support a mission.

Mission of the Church

THEOLOGICAL INTRODUCTION

Q. For what special role in the Church did Jesus choose Peter?
"The Lord made Simon alone, whom he named Peter, the 'rock' of his Church. He gave him the keys of his Church, and instituted him shepherd of the whole flock. 'The office of binding and loosing which was given to Peter was also assigned to the college of apostles united to its head.' This pastoral office of Peter and the other apostles belongs to the Church's very foundation and is continued by the bishops under the primacy of the Pope" (*CCC 881*).

Q. What mission did Jesus give to his followers?
"So that this call should resound throughout the world, Christ sent forth the apostles he had chosen, commissioning them to proclaim the gospel: 'Go therefore and make disciples of all nations, baptising them in the name of the Father and of the Son and of the Holy Spirit, teaching them to observe all that I have commanded you; and lo, I am with you always, to the close of the age.' Strengthened by this mission, the apostles 'went forth and preached everywhere, while the Lord worked with them and confirmed the message by the signs that attended it'" (*CCC 2*).

"At last Jesus' hour arrives: he commends his spirit into the Father's hands... From this hour onwards, the mission of the Christ and the Spirit becomes the mission of the Church: 'As the Father has sent me, even so I send you'" (*CCC 730, see also 737*). "To proclaim the faith and to plant his reign, Christ sends his apostles and their successors. He gives them a share in his own mission. From him they receive the power to act in his person" (*CCC 935*).

Q. What happened at Pentecost?
"On the day of Pentecost when the seven weeks of Easter had come to an end, Christ's Passover is fulfilled in the outpouring of the Holy Spirit, manifested, given and communicated as a divine person: of his fullness, Christ, the Lord, pours out the Spirit in abundance" (*CCC 731*). "'When the work which the Father gave the Son to do on earth was accomplished, the Holy Spirit was sent on the day of Pentecost in order that he might continually sanctify the Church.' Then 'the Church was openly displayed to the crowds and the spread of the Gospel among the nations, through preaching, was begun.' As the 'convocation' of all men for salvation, the Church in her very nature is missionary, sent by Christ to all the nations to make disciples of them" (*CCC 767*). "The Church was made manifest to the world on the day of Pentecost by the outpouring of the Holy Spirit..." (*CCC 1076*).

Q. How did St Peter fulfil his mission?
On the day of Pentecost Peter stood up with the eleven and addressed a crowd that had gathered. As a witness to the resurrection he proclaimed Jesus and invited his hearers to repent of their unbelief. That very day about three thousand were added to the Church (*Acts 2*). He worked miracles of healing and continued to preach in Jerusalem (*Acts 3*).

With the other apostles Peter was persecuted by the Jews, but continued to preach the Good News both in the Temple and in private houses (*Acts 4 and 5*). He preached in Lydda and cured a paralytic there and converted many. At Jaffa he raised the dead widow Tabitha, or Dorcas in Greek, to life and many in Jaffa came to believe because of the miracle (*Acts 9*). In obedience to a vision he went to preach to the gentile centurion of the Italica cohort, Cornelius who was stationed in Caesarea. He and all his household accepted the Good News and became Christians (*Acts 10*). He was imprisoned by king Herod but miraculously freed (*Acts 12*).

Mission of the Church

He spoke with authority at the meeting in Jerusalem to decide whether converts should also keep all the Jewish precepts. With the other apostles and leaders of the Church, Peter approved the ruling of the assembly and signed the apostolic letter promulgated by them (*Acts 15*).

St Jerome, Eusebius, St Chrysostom and other ancient writers assure us that he was bishop in Antioch for about seven years, from 33AD to 40AD. He founded the Church in Rome and was bishop in Rome for many years. Ancient writers say for 25 years. Two letters of St Peter are in the New Testament. The first is his but the second seems to date later than his death and was perhaps written by someone who could claim to represent him. He was crucified for the faith during the persecutions of Christians by the emperor Nero in 65AD. There is a tradition that he was crucified upside down at his own request because he was too humble to be as Christ on the cross. Thus he completed his mission as the first of the apostles.

Q. What happened to St Stephen and why?
Stephen, a man full of faith and of the Holy Spirit, was elected a deacon, with six others, to help with the distribution of alms in the first Christian community in Jerusalem. Filled with grace and power he began to work miracles and great signs among the people. In his zeal for the Good News he debated with Jews from Cyrene and Alexandria, members of the Synagogue of Freedmen, (probably Jews who had been freed from slavery.) They could not get the better of him because of his wisdom and because of the Spirit who prompted what he said. They, therefore, falsely accused him and he was stoned to death, the first to die for preaching the Good News (*Acts 6 and 7*).

Q. How did Saul come to be called Paul and how did he spread the Good News?
Some think that Saul took the name Paul from the proconsul Sergius Paulus (*cf. Acts 13*). Others think he changed his name to Paul at his conversion.

Barnabus brought Saul to Antioch to help found the Church there (*Acts 11*). Because of a revelation of the Holy Spirit, the Church at Antioch commissioned Barnabus and Paul to preach the Good News to other cities. They made their first missionary journey together and established local churches in Asia Minor. St Paul split from Barnabus and made two further missionary journeys founding churches in Macedonia and Greece (*Acts 13 to 21*). Then he went up to Jerusalem. The Jews conspired to kill him, but his nephew was warned about it. He told the centurion of the plot and was sent under escort to Caesarea.

After two years under house arrest he appealed to be tried by Ceasar and was taken to Rome. There, under house arrest, he continued to preach to all who came to see him. After two years he was released and continued his missionary journeys. Back in Rome he suffered death by being beheaded under the persecution of Nero. He wrote letters to the churches he founded and these make up a treasured part of the New Testament.

Q. How are we called to share in the Church's mission?
"Those who with God's help have welcomed Christ's call and freely responded to it are urged on by the love of Christ to proclaim the Good News everywhere in the world. This treasure, received from the apostles, has been faithfully guarded by their successors. All Christ's faithful are called to hand it on from generation to generation, by professing the faith, by living it in fraternal sharing, and by celebrating it in liturgy and prayer" (*CCC 3*).

Mission of the Church

Summary

All members of the Church are called to proclaim the Good News that "when the appointed time came, God sent his Son, born of a woman, born a subject of the Law, to redeem the subjects of the Law and enable them to be adopted as sons" (*Galatians 4:4-5*).

POINTS FOR DISCUSSION AND FURTHER ACTIVITIES

LEARNING OBJECTIVE: know that Peter was chosen by Jesus to lead the disciples in the mission to spread the Good News

Discussion
- Talk about Peter's sorrow for what he had done to let Jesus down. Why do the children think he was sorry? Was it because he thought Jesus would be angry, or not be his friend any more? Or was he genuinely sorry that he had broken the friendship and hurt Jesus?
- Discuss briefly the meaning of 'mission'. What do the pupils understand by a 'mission'? Who do we think has a mission today? (*Priests, teachers, doctors etc.*)
- When Jesus asked Peter to feed his lambs and his sheep, what did he mean? Who are the lambs and sheep? How was Peter to feed them? What with? Who are the sheep and lambs now? Who feeds them now?

Activities
- St Peter is often shown in pictures with a set of keys. Find and read Matthew 16:18-19. What was the promise Jesus made to Peter then? Write out verse 19 and draw St Peter with the keys.

LEARNING OBJECTIVE: know that the Church began at Pentecost when Jesus sent his Holy Spirit to help his disciples

Information

The Jewish Feast of Pentecost

It was the day of the Jewish feast of Pentecost when the Holy Spirit came to give the Apostles strength and courage. Jerusalem was full of people who had come from near and far for the feast. It was one of the most important feasts for the Jewish people. The Feast of Pentecost came 50 days after Passover - Pentecost is Greek for '50 days'. Sometimes it was called the 'Feast of Weeks' as it came on the day after 49 days after Passover (7 times 7 days.) Passover was the beginning of the grain harvest and Pentecost was the end of it, so it was a kind of harvest festival for the first fruits of the grain harvest.

We call Pentecost the 'Birthday of the Church'; it is like a harvest as well - a harvest of the fruits of Jesus' love for humanity. Later on, the Jews always remembered the giving of the Law to Moses at this feast, and thought of the covenant God had made with them.

Discussion
- Ask the pupils to think about the days between the Ascension of Jesus into Heaven and Pentecost, when the Holy Spirit came. Where were they? Who were they with? What did they do? How do the pupils prepare for an important event they are waiting for? Do they pray?

Mission of the Church

- How do the children imagine the Holy Spirit? Do they remember any of the symbols we use to talk about him? (Dove, wind, fire, cloud and light) No-one can see the Holy Spirit - because he is a spirit and spirits can't be seen - but everyone can see and know the effects of his work. Remind the children that the Apostles heard a sound like a great wind when the Holy Spirit came - perhaps they remembered the words of Jesus about the Holy Spirit in John 3:8.

Activities
- In pairs, draw or paint a picture of the Apostles before and after the Holy Spirit came to them. Show how they felt and acted quite differently before and after the coming of the Holy Spirit.
- Make a Pentecost display, with large red flickering-flame shapes as the background. Make the heads of the Apostles to go under them, perhaps with painted blown eggs to link with Easter. Paint large coloured words such as 'courage' or 'hope' or 'strength' to go with the Apostles.

LEARNING OBJECTIVE: know how St Peter and St Stephen helped to spread the Good News by their lives and deaths

Peter was arrested and escaped with the help of an angel (*Adapted from Acts 12:1-18*)
The Apostles had already been arrested and put in prison at least once for teaching about Jesus - and an angel had released them. Now another time of trouble came along for them. This time, Herod the king captured James the brother of John and killed him. Then he arrested Peter and put him in prison, with four squads of soldiers to guard him. While Peter was in prison, the whole Church prayed very hard to God for him.

One night, Peter was fast asleep, with a soldier on each side of him, and chains on his hands and feet. There were even sentries guarding the door. Suddenly, a light shone in that dark place and an angel appeared - an angel of the Lord. The angel tapped Peter on the side to wake him up.

"Get up quickly," the angel said, "Get dressed, put on your cloak and sandals and follow me!"

Peter thought he was seeing a vision - he didn't think it was really happening - so he did as the angel said.

They passed the first guard, they passed the second guard and they came to the iron gate leading into the city. The gate opened to them on its own and they went out. They walked along one street and then the angel disappeared. Peter realised at last what was happening - it was all real and he was free!

"Now I know that the Lord has sent his angel and rescued me," he said to himself. When he realised this, he went straight away to the house where he knew his friends were gathered to pray for him. When he knocked at the gate, a maid came to see who it was. As soon as she saw it was Peter, she was so delighted, she ran back to tell everyone so quickly that she forgot to open the gate and let Peter in! Of course, everyone thought she was mad. "You've seen a ghost!" they said. But Peter went on knocking at the gate until at last they went to see who was there. Then they had to believe it!

Mission of the Church

Discussion
- Peter had an important job to do and Jesus was not going to let him die until he had done it. When he was in prison, it must have seemed to him that all was lost and finished. Yet he was sleeping when the angel came - not lying awake worrying. Have the children experienced times when it was hard to trust that God is really in charge? How do they think Peter managed to trust that everything would be all right?
- Peter's friends were praying for him, and their prayers were answered. They were very happy about this. But what if Peter's time on earth had been finished, as happened later when he was martyred? How would his friends have felt then? Would they still have trusted in God? How do the children feel when it seems their prayers have not been answered? Do they remember God is still in charge?

Activities
- When Stephen was martyred for his faith in Jesus - that means, he was killed for being a witness to the truth about Jesus - he looked up to heaven as he was dying. Read Acts 7:55-56 and describe what he saw.
- Research some other martyrs for the Catholic faith. Choose one and prepare a talk for the class on his/her life.

LEARNING OBJECTIVE: know how Saul became Paul and worked to spread the Good News

Discussion
- When Saul was on the way to Damascus to capture Christians, he heard Jesus asking, "Why are you persecuting me?" How was Saul persecuting Jesus? Are there times in our lives when we persecute Jesus?
- God intervened in very dramatic ways in the early days of the Church. He sent an angel to rescue Peter and Jesus himself appeared to Saul. This shows the importance of their tasks. Tell the children how Peter came to Rome and was martyred there, and that there is a large Church there bearing his name. Do the children know that Peter was the first Pope, or leader/father of the Church on earth and that the leader of the Church on earth now is still in Rome? Do they know the name of our Pope now?
- Talk to the children about Simon and Saul, who became Peter and Paul, and how their characters as well as their names changed with the jobs they had to do for Jesus.
- Tell the children that Paul travelled far and wide within the Roman Empire to spread the Good News about Jesus, and that he founded the Church in many towns. When he left, he wrote letters to these towns, and some of these letters are now part of our Bible. They come after the Gospels and the Acts of the Apostles.

Activities
- Imagine you are Paul and you have arrived in a town where they have never heard of Jesus. What will you tell the people? How will you explain who Jesus is? Write down or tell the class the important points you think they should know. The rest of the class can decide, when they have heard what you have to say, whether you have convinced them to believe in Jesus or not.

ICT
www.kolbenet.com/kolbe/   Story of St Maximilian Kolbe
www.adena.com/adena/sts/barbara.htm   Story of St Barbara
www.netaxs.com/~rmk/saints.html   Saints stories, written by children
www.ainglkiss.com/apo/   The Twelve Apostles

6 BELONGING TO THE CHURCH

"[The Church] is the People of God... drawn into Christ's praise of the Father and Christ's mission in the world. The Church is the holy people of God, the communion of saints... The saints who have entered through death into God's glory are united in Christ with the saints on earth through faith and charity." (RECD p.19)

"[Baptism is one of the] sacraments of Christian initiation which lay the foundations of every Christian life. In Baptism we are reborn as children of God in Christ and enlightened by the Holy Spirit. In Confirmation the laying on of hands and anointing with oil are the seal of the Holy Spirit which marks our total belonging to Christ and to his service." (RECD p.24)

Key learning objectives:

AT 1
In this unit you will have the opportunity to:

- know what a community is and that there are different types of community;

- understand what it means to belong to the community of the Church;

- have some understanding of the Creed as a statement of our faith;

- know that the creed is an expression of these beliefs and vision;

- know that we 'join' the Church community when we are baptised;

- know that we mark our total belonging to Christ when we receive the Sacrament of Confirmation.

AT 2
You will have the chance to:

- reflect on the different communities to which we belong;

- reflect on the joys and challenges of belonging to a community;

- explore how we show commitment to our communities;

- reflect on ways we 'joined' some of the communities.

Belonging to the Church

THEOLOGICAL INTRODUCTION

Q. What is a community?
Q. What different types of community are there?
A community is a group of people with a common interest. Some are natural communities such as the family and the groups of families and of people who make up a society. Others are formed by people who want, for instance, to protect the environment or help the poor. Some are religious communities such as monks and nuns. Some communities are called into existence by God's choice. The chosen people, the Jews, are such a community as is the Catholic Church.

Q. What does belonging to the community of the Church mean?
"Fully incorporated into the society of the Church are those who, possessing the Spirit of Christ, accept all the means of salvation given to the Church together with her entire organisation, and who - by the bonds constituted by the profession of faith, the sacraments, ecclesiastical government, and communion - are joined in the visible structure of the Church of Christ, who rules her through the Supreme Pontiff and the bishops" (*CCC 837*).

Q. What are Creeds?
Q. How do Creeds unite us together in the Church?
"Whoever says 'I believe' says 'I pledge myself to what *we* believe.' Communion in faith needs a common language of faith, normative for all and uniting all in the same confession of faith" (*CCC 185*). "From the beginning, the apostolic Church expressed and handed on her faith in brief formulae normative for all. But already very early on, the Church also wanted to gather the essential elements of her faith into organic and articulated summaries, intended especially for candidates for Baptism:

"This synthesis of faith [the creed] was not made to accord with human opinion, but rather what was of the greatest importance was gathered from all the Scriptures, to present the one teaching of the faith in its entirety. And just as the mustard seed contains a great number of branches in a tiny grain, so too this summary of faith encompassed in a few words the whole knowledge of the true religion contained in the Old and New Testaments" (*CCC 186*).

"Such syntheses are called 'professions of faith' since they summarise the faith that Christians profess. They are called 'creeds' on account of what is usually their first word in Latin: *credo* ('I believe'). They are also called 'symbols of faith'" (*CCC 187*). "The Greek word *symbolon* meant half of a broken object, for example, a seal presented as a token of recognition. The broken parts were placed together to verify the bearer's identity. The symbol of faith, then, is a sign of recognition and communion between believers. *Symbol* also means a gathering, collection or summary. A symbol of faith is a summary of the principal truths of the faith and therefore serves as the first and fundamental point of reference for catechesis" (*CCC 188*).

Q. How do we join the Church community?
"Baptism makes us members of the Body of Christ: 'Therefore... we are members one of another.' Baptism incorporates us *into the Church*. From the baptismal fonts is born the one People of God of the New Covenant, which transcends all the natural or human limits of nations, cultures, races and sexes: 'For by one Spirit we were all baptised into one body.'" (*CCC 1267*).

Belonging to the Church

Q. What is the effect of the Sacrament of Confirmation?

"Confirmation perfects Baptismal grace; it is the sacrament which gives the Holy Spirit in order to root us more deeply in the divine filiation, incorporate us more firmly into Christ, strengthen our bond with the Church, associate us more closely with her mission, and help us bear witness to the Christian faith in words accompanied by deeds" (*CCC 1316*).

Q. What do we celebrate on the Feast of All Saints (*November 1st*)**?**

"After confessing 'the Holy Catholic Church', the Apostles' creed adds 'the communion of saints'. In a certain sense this article is a further explanation of the preceding: 'What is the Church if not the assembly of all the saints?' The communion of saints is the Church" (*CCC 946*).

"*The three states of the Church.* 'When the Lord comes in glory, and all the angels with him, death will be no more and all things will be subject to him. But at the present time some of his disciples are pilgrims on earth. Others have died and are being purified, while still others are in glory, contemplating 'in full light, God himself triune and one, exactly as he is:'"

"All of us, however, in varying degrees and in different ways share in the same charity towards God and our neighbours, and we all sing the one hymn of glory to our God. All, indeed, who are of Christ and who have his Spirit form one Church and in Christ cleave together" (*CCC 954*).

The Feast of All Saints celebrates this wonderful communion of the saints in Christ.

Summary

By Baptism we become part of the body of Christ, which is the Church. By Confirmation we are confirmed in that union. The Church was created to be Christ to the world. The mission of the Church is live as Christ did in the world. This is made possible for us by God's grace. It is for us to accord with his grace and love one another as he loved us. To be a member of the Church is to be called to live as saints.

POINTS FOR DISCUSSION AND FURTHER ACTIVITIES

LEARNING OBJECTIVE: know that you belong to a community

Discussion

- What is the most important community to which the children belong? For most, it will be the family, though sensitivity is necessary when discussing this with children who may be bereft of all or part of their close family.

Activities

- Ask the children to say why they think their parents sent them to a Catholic school. What do they think their parents hoped for them to gain from going to their particular school? This could be a class discussion, or each child could write down their reasons which could be compared. How well do the children think the school lives up to these hopes?

Belonging to the Church

- Work in pairs or small groups. Talk about anything about which you would like to ask God's help or blessing - these could be either personal or world issues. Then each child writes a short prayer for the other person's intentions.

Learning Objective: know that there are different types of communities

Discussion
- Talk about the different communities to which the children belong - what are the aims of these communities - how do the children contribute towards these aims?

Activities
- Find out about some communities which exist to benefit others. Perhaps there are some in your town? Most towns now have some kind of website which may have a link, or there may be an Information Centre in larger towns.
- Look up and read Acts 4:32-35. This tells you about the first Christian community - the early Church. Explain in your own words what happened in this community.

Learning Objective: know what it means to belong to the community of the Church

Discussion
- Ask the children if there are any ways in which they serve the Church community where they worship. Perhaps some serve on the altar, sing in the choir, play instruments... or perhaps they help in other ways - serving coffee after Mass, tidying up or helping with younger children. Draw attention to the fact that there are those who serve simply by being there and behaving well.

Learning Objective: know that we join the Church when we are Baptised

Discussion (*Be aware that some pupils may not (yet) be Baptised*)
- Ask the children to say what happens at a Baptism and help them to remember the visible signs, e.g. water, white garment, chrism and candle. Remind them that Baptism is a sacrament. Ask them if they remember what happens at Baptism, that the Holy Spirit comes to live in them and give them God's own life, and that they are now members of the Church - God's children and brothers and sisters of Jesus.

Activities
- In groups, use a large piece of paper to draw a big 'church' shape - perhaps you could think of the outline of your own Church building. Inside the shape, draw or paint some small pictures showing 'snapshots' from the community life of the Catholic Church. You could use a scene from any of the seven sacraments, from the Mass, from Benediction, or any other time when the Church community is together. Can you think of a suitable 'theme' to join your pictures - trailing vine stems, perhaps? Or linked hands? Or a chain?

Belonging to the Church

LEARNING OBJECTIVE: know that the Creed states what we believe

Discussion
- Explain briefly to the children that the 'Communion of Saints' to which we all belong is the whole Church community, past present and future. Some of us are living here and now, doing our best to live according to the new life we received in Baptism and receiving God's help and forgiveness when we fail. Some Christians lived long ago (or more recently) and have died - their souls may already be in heaven - we call them **Saints** - and we can ask them to pray for us. They are good role models, but also helpers. Some Christians are waiting to enter their life with God - we call these the **Holy Souls** and **we** can help **them** by praying for them. We do this in November especially.

Activity
- Write a prayer to one of the saints in heaven, asking them to pray for you.

LEARNING OBJECTIVE: know about the important celebrations in the Church

Discussion
- Why do the children think the liturgical colours were chosen for those times of the Church's year? What do the colours white, red, green, purple make them think of? Have they ever seen red vestments? Or pink, or blue?
- Explain to the children that as well as celebrating Advent, Christmas, Lent, Easter and so on every year, we also celebrate other feasts on their proper days, which can be confusing. For instance, often in the middle of Lent, when we are thinking about Jesus being tempted in the dessert, or about his betrayal and death, we stop to celebrate the Annunciation - when the angel Gabriel came to Mary. We fit it all in every year!

Activities
- As well as the priest's vestments, other things in the Church use the liturgical colours. Working in groups, try to remember what else you have seen in the Church with the same colours (tabernacle veil, lectern, altar frontal). In your groups, or alone, draw one of these in one of the liturgical colours. Write beside it what it is (a description will do if you can't remember the name) and what season of the Church's year it is for.
- Make a design for use in Church (perhaps on the altar frontal or on the lectern). Use one of the liturgical colours for the background and choose an appropriate symbol or simplified picture to go on the foreground. Perhaps you would be able to make your design from fabric and use it in school.

ICT
www.angelfire.com/oh2/stcyprian/seasons.html   A good site for teachers to find information on the seasons of the Church's year
www.catholicism.about.com/cs/symbols   Five pages of Catholic clip art by Fr Richard Lonsdale & Christian symbols by Rudolf Kock

Index for Photocopy Worksheets

The Bible - Photocopy Worksheets
Moses and the Exodus 44
David and Goliath 47
Jonah 50
The Bible is a story about God's love for us 56
God speaks to us in the Bible 57
Finding your way around the Bible 58

Trust in God - Photocopy Worksheets
St Joseph trusted in God 59
Mary's Song of Praise - The Magnificat 60
Christmas Cards 62
The Flight into Egypt 63
Know how Joseph put his trust in God... 64

Jesus, the Teacher - Photocopy Worksheets
Jewish Worship of God 65
Jesus shows us how to live 66
Know the teaching of Jesus 67
The Great Feast 68
The Parable of the Sower 69

Jesus, the Saviour - Photocopy Worksheets
Good Friday 70
Holy Week: What happened when? 72
Holy Week 73
Easter Liturgy 74

Mission of the Church - Photocopy Worksheets
Prayers to the Holy Spirit 75
Peter and Paul 76
What can we do to prepare for our mission? 77
Our Parish Church Project 78

MOSES and the EXODUS

I have a story to tell - a story of the miracles the God of the Israelites can do. And not just little disappearing tricks or illusions - oh no. I mean totally amazing, mind-blowing, life-changing miracles. Let me tell you what happened.

It all started when this one Israelite called **Moses** decided his people had been badly treated by the Egyptians for too long. Well, he said it wasn't his decision: it was God's. So he went along to the King of Egypt - Pharaoh - and demanded that he let his people go. Now, this was quite something. For one thing, usually no one could get within a hundred meters of Pharaoh but - well, Moses was determined and, to give him his due, he succeeded. But let's face it: the chances of Pharaoh releasing the Israelites were remote. They were the Egyptians' slaves. They were used as labourers for building great cities. Did Moses seriously think Pharaoh would just say: Sure, off you go, we'll just do all the work ourselves? And then, there was Moses' own problem. He was shy. He wasn't too good with words either. So he was hardly going to persuade Pharaoh to let the Israelites go, was he?

Well, that's when the plagues started, as we called them at the time. Each time Moses went along to Pharaoh with his demand, and each time Pharaoh refused. And so, God did everything possible to give Pharaoh a chance to change his mind. First, the water in all the rivers and ponds and canals turned to blood! Urgh! "Let the people go!" Moses demanded. "No!" replied Pharaoh. So along came another plague - frogs, millions upon millions of them, hopping all over the land. Then another - gnats; then flies, swarms of them everywhere. Nine times Moses went to Pharaoh and told him it was the will of God that the Israelites should be released. And each time, the King of the Egyptians refused. There were more plagues - all the cattle died, then everyone developed boils, then there were huge hailstones, then swarms of locusts that ate every bit of the crops; then the lights went out. Well, that's what it seemed like. There was darkness over the whole of Egypt for three whole days. No sun, no moon, no stars, nothing! Still Pharaoh remained stubborn.

"Very well!" said God. "I've given Pharaoh nine chances - nine warnings. This time he will let the Israelites go!" God had given Pharaoh every chance possible, but still he would not do as God asked. So God told Moses to give his people these instructions:

"Get ready for a long journey. But before we go, we're going to eat a special meal: roast lamb with herbs and bread baked without yeast. The blood of the lamb needs to be sprinkled round our doors. Because tonight, God's going to pass over Egypt and all of the oldest children are going to die. But when he sees blood on the door-frames, he'll pass over those houses because he'll know that they belong to us - to the Israelites."

So that's what happened. God had tried everything before sending this, the tenth and most horrible plague. But Pharaoh refused to listen. And of course, whose son also died on that night? That's right, Pharaoh's! Well, you can imagine how he felt, can't you? "Get out of here!" he screamed at Moses. "Take your people and go! I never want to see any of you again. Your God is too powerful for me to resist any longer!"

The Israelites were ready. Their bags were packed, they had their walking shoes on their feet, they'd even had a good meal to give them strength for their journey. They moved! Men, women and children, goats, sheep and cows, all headed out of Egypt - until they reached the Red Sea on Egypt's eastern border. But by this time, Pharaoh had had time to think about what had happened. He was still grieving for his dead son, but now he was angry too. "No! I want them back!" his voice echoed around his palace. "Get my chariot ready ... and my whole army. We're going after them!" Six hundred of his finest chariots thundered out of the city - followed by all his soldiers and horses. The Israelites on the shore of the Red Sea could see the dust rising on the horizon as they got nearer.

"What have you done, Moses?" they cried. "We were better off in Egypt. But now we're going to die!"

And that's when the next great miracle happened. "Raise your hand over the sea," God told Moses. Moses raised his hand over the water and the Red Sea divided. It wasn't a bridge. It wasn't a tunnel. It was a great dry route right through the middle of the sea.

"Come on!" someone shouted, and the Israelites surged forward, families and all their possessions, passing through the Red Sea, heading for freedom, for safety, for their own land as God had promised them.

Photocopy Worksheets - The Bible

The Egyptians were close behind them, though. They saw them passing through the sea and Pharaoh ordered his army to follow. The chariots, the horses, the foot soldiers thundered into the channel and, just as they reached the middle of the Red Sea, the last Israelites were reaching the far shore.

"Put out your hand over the water again," God ordered Moses. And Moses obeyed. The waters filled up again, pouring over the Egyptians, destroying the entire army, until not a single soldier remained.

Yes indeed, those were amazing times. We saw the hand of God at work. The Israelites had prayed to him, asking him to deliver them from the Egyptians; and he answered their prayers. And despite what seemed like impossible odds, he did rescue his people and bring them safely out of Egypt. After seeing miracles like that - the plagues, the Passover, and the parting of the Red Sea - is it any wonder I believe in him? Oh yes, by the way, I did actually see those miracles ... because I was one of the Israelites who escaped that night.

Activities

1. Why did Moses go to the King of Egypt?

2. Were the Israelites treated well in Egypt?

3. What type of a man was Moses?

4. Describe some of the plagues.

5. What was it that persuaded Pharaoh to let the Israelites go free?

6. Describe how the Israelites got across the Red Sea.

7. Why couldn't the Egyptians follow them?

Photocopy Worksheets - The Bible

David and Goliath

As told by Joachim, a soldier in King Saul's army

My fellow soldiers and I sat around the fire feeling very sad. Our army had been fighting the Philistines for months, but we never seemed to be winning. Every time we attacked them, they fought back, usually gaining some more ground. We had lost many men and it seemed as though we were never going to beat them.

"It's that champion of theirs," said Benjamin. "He's just too powerful!"
"He's not just too powerful," chipped in Gad. "He's too big!" We laughed, but Gad was right. Goliath was big - a giant of a man. He towered over our soldiers, swinging his sword from left to right, and we stood no chance. Some of us had volunteered to fight him, but no one had been strong enough to beat him.

Suddenly, Tobiah ran past our group. "Quickly!" he shouted excitedly. "Get down to the plain. Someone else is going to fight Goliath!"

"Who is it?" We asked, jumping up and following him. Tobiah couldn't hide the laughter in his voice as he replied: "David!"

We looked at each other in disbelief. David! But he was only a boy - a shepherd boy, at that! He'd been invited to the court of King Saul as a musician. Everyone liked him but he was no soldier. Surely Tobiah had been mistaken.

But no. When we reached the hillside overlooking the plain, there he was. And what a ridiculous sight he made! He was wearing great heavy armour, a helmet and breastplate. He was sagging beneath the weight of a shield and sword. We stopped laughing and felt really disappointed. There was no way that this boy could beat the Philistines' giant!

"Please," I heard him say to one of the soldiers. "Take this off me. I don't need this armour. I'm not used to it"

"But it's the king's own armour. And besides, you're going to fight Goliath!" the soldier replied. David ignored him and struggled to free himself from the breastplate, until he stood in only his tunic. He looked so small and fragile. Then I noticed someone behind him: King Saul himself.

"So how will you fight, David, without weapons or armour?" he said to the boy.

Photocopy Worksheets - The Bible

"I have God, Your Majesty," he answered. "He will protect me. He will be my shield and my sword. As long as God is on our side, no one can harm us." Saul smiled faintly and put his hand on David's shoulder.

"Then may God be with you," he said.

"He is," David told him. "With me, with you, and with the people of Israel - his people!" And with that, the shepherd boy turned and strode into the middle of the plain calling Goliath's name.

The Philistine army started to cheer as the earth shook and their champion appeared. He looked even bigger in his armour, a gleaming sword in his massive hand, and he towered over young David. It seemed so unfair that the boy would be killed; I wanted to turn away, it was almost too awful to watch. But I stayed and saw him pull something from his belt: a sling - a sort of catapult. Then he bent down and started to pick up pebbles from the rocky ground. What on earth was he doing?

The Israelite army - my army - fell silent, watching David. But the Philistines roared with laughter. As if it hadn't been enough for us to send a boy out to fight their champion, now it looked like he was playing stones on the valley floor! Goliath too laughed - a deep, awful laugh, and swung his sword above his head.

"What do you think I am? A dog? You're just a boy with sticks!" he bellowed. But David stared into his eyes, no fear on his face, only a look of determination. Then his young voice echoed over the plain:

"I stand before you in the name of the Lord, the God of the Israelites' army. Today, he will make me strong, and hand you over to us. I will strike you down, Goliath, and cut off your head. And everyone here will know that the Lord is stronger than any sword or armour; the battle will be won by him!"

All eyes were on David as he placed one of the pebbles in his sling and swung it faster and faster over his head, until it became a blur. Then, with one great final swing, he threw the stone in the direction of the giant's face. The armies gasped as it flew through the air with a high pitched whistling sound, and struck Goliath right between the eyes: "Whack!" For a moment, everything was still and quiet. No one moved. Even Goliath himself remained still, his sword held high above his head. Next moment, he started to sway. He crumpled to his knees and then keeled over. The ground shook as he fell: dead.

Suddenly, an enormous cheer went up from the Israelites and we ran onto the plain. We surged around David, patting him on the back. Then we lifted him onto our shoulders and carried him back to the camp, singing.

"The Lord God guards and protects us: great is the Lord!
He saves his people, Israel, and overcomes our enemies.
The Lord is our fortress and our strength, our shield and our sword.
Blessed be David who trusted God and defeated the giant!"

Activities

1. What was David like?

2. How was he going to fight the giant?

3. What did the people think would happen to David?

4. Who do you think helped David to win the battle?

JONAH

CAST: God   Narrator   Merchant 1   Sailor 1
Jonah   Merchant 2   Sailor 2

Merchant 1   Welcome to the city of Nineveh - the richest, most powerful city in the world! And the biggest: it will take you three days to walk from one side of the city to the other!

Merchant 2   People from all over the world visit our market here in Nineveh. They come to buy our beautiful cloth - fine silks from Asia - and to enjoy our exotic foods: strange spices, almonds and raisins that come from faraway lands.

Narrator   But the people of Nineveh were wicked. They were selfish and greedy; they stole from each other and they didn't worship God properly. Even their king ignored the needs of his people. He spent all his time eating and drinking and wearing expensive robes in his palace. God wanted to help them change their ways, so he decided to send Jonah.

God   Jonah, Jonah!

Jonah   Yes, God.

God   Go to the people of Nineveh and tell them I'm very angry with them. Tell them to change their ways and to start caring for each other. Otherwise, I shall punish them.

Jonah   But ... I can't do that! They are so wicked they don't deserve to be saved. I shan't go to Nineveh. I'm going to run away and hide.

Narrator	So, the next day, he headed for the harbour and found a boat that was about to set sail.
Jonah	Hello! Would you mind taking me with you?
Sailor 1	Alright - if you are prepared to pay the fare. Come on board.
Narrator	So Jonah climbed aboard and they set sail.
Jonah	This is great! I didn't want to go to Nineveh, and here I am, on a boat heading somewhere else. God won't be able to find me here.
Narrator	But after a while, the wind began to blow and rain began to fall. The boat was tossed up and down on the enormous waves. The sailors had never seen such bad weather. They tried to steer the boat with oars, but the storm was too fierce. They were helpless.
Sailor 2	If the storm gets any worse, our boat will sink! We'll all be drowned!
Sailor 1	Let's throw the cargo overboard. If we make the boat lighter, we might be able to ride the storm.
Narrator	But throwing the cargo overboard didn't help. The storm got worse. Water flooded the deck. The waves got bigger. The wind got stronger.
Sailor 2	God must be angry with us. But why? What have we done?
Jonah	I know why. This is all my fault. God is angry with me. Listen: God told me to go to Nineveh, to tell the people

Photocopy Worksheets - The Bible

there to change their ways. But I refused. I ran away from God and didn't do as he said. But the storm will end if you throw me overboard. Then you will be safe.

Sailors Are you sure, Jonah? Must we really throw you overboard?

Jonah Yes, I am sure.

Narrator So the sailor did as Jonah said. They lifted him up, carried him to the side of the boat and dropped him into the water. He sank like a stone and disappeared beneath the waves.

Immediately, the wind dropped, and the rain stopped. The sea became calm and the storm was over. The ship was safe once more, just as Jonah had said it would be.

Jonah Help! I can't swim. My mouth and nose are filling up with salty water. In another minute, I will be dead ...

Narrator But just then something odd happened. Jonah couldn't see much in the dark water, but an enormous shape swept up to him from below. He felt himself sucked into a tunnel, and hurled over and over until he was dizzy. Eventually, he landed on the soft floor of what seemed to be a sort of cave.

Jonah Where am I? It's so dark and it smells horrible! Stale fish! There's rotting seaweed everywhere. And the floor is all wet! And ... oh no! It can't be true! It's impossible! I've been swallowed by a great fish!

Narrator Yes, Jonah was inside the belly of a great fish. He had been swallowed alive. And that's where he stayed for three days and three nights. That gave him plenty of time to think and to pray.

Jonah	I'm sorry, God. I shouldn't have disobeyed you. I've learnt my lesson. If you still want me to go to Nineveh, I will. I'll do anything you ask.
God	Well, Jonah, if you are truly sorry, I will let you out. Are you sure you will go to Nineveh? You won't try to run away and hide from me again, will you?
Jonah	No, I promise.
Narrator	The enormous fish swam close to the shore and headed for the surface. As it raised its head above the water, it yawned and then coughed. Jonah was hurled out of his mouth and into the air. With a thud, he landed on the beach.
Jonah	Ouch! But at least this is better than being inside the big fish. The sun feels great on my shoulders; the sand is warm and dry; and, mmm, fresh air! Oh, this is lovely.
God	This is no time for sunbathing, Jonah. You made me a promise. Up you get! Go to Nineveh and tell the people to change their bad ways. And remember, if they don't, then I will punish them; I will destroy their beautiful city.
Narrator	So Jonah got up and headed straight for Nineveh. When he arrived there, he stood in the middle of the marketplace and they all gathered round to hear him.
Jonah	People of Nineveh, listen to me. God has been watching you. He has seen your wicked ways. He knows how you cheat and lie and steal.
Merchant 1	Really? God has been watching that?

Photocopy Worksheets - The Bible

Jonah	Yes - and he wants you to change your ways. To start caring for each other, showing kindness and love. God is a loving, forgiving God. But he does not ignore injustice and evil. So, if you refuse to change...
Merchant 2	Yes? If we refuse...?
Jonah	If you refuse, if you do not change your wicked ways, God will punish you.
Merchant 2	How?
Jonah	God will destroy Nineveh!
Merchant 1	No, Jonah, please! We will change! God doesn't need to destroy our beautiful city - we will stop being so wicked.
Merchant 2	Yes, we will fast for a week: we won't eat anything at all, to show God we really mean it. And we will wear rags instead of our rich robes to show him we are truly sorry.
Merchants	We believe that God is a God who forgives.
Narrator	And God saw that the people of Nineveh really did mean what they said, so he forgave them. They changed their ways and started worshipping as he wanted, so he didn't destroy their city.
Jonah	Even though they deserved it!
God	What was that, Jonah?

Jonah I said: even though they deserved it. I knew this would happen. Why did you forgive them, God? They were wicked: they didn't deserve to be saved.

God But Jonah, they heard my message from you; and they believed you. They changed their ways. Wouldn't you rather I forgive people when they are truly sorry?

Jonah Well...

God After all, I forgave you and saved you when you were inside the belly of the big fish, didn't I?

Jonah Well, yes, I suppose so.

God And that's because I am a loving forgiving God, just like you told the people of Nineveh. Right?

Narrator And Jonah remembered what it had been like inside the big fish, and the smell, and the water. And he remembered how God had forgiven him and saved him. And he had to agree.

Photocopy Worksheets - The Bible

The Bible is a story about God's love for us

Activities

1. Complete the story in the box, use the words below to help you.

2. Choose two important words from the box and explain why they are important.

The Bible tells us that God is _____ because he made the whole universe. We are his children, and that is why we call him our _____. God protects us, so we call him a _____. He gave us _____ to help us live happily and peacefully together. God _____ us when we sin because he loves us. He cares for us like a _____. God loved the world so much, he gave us his only _____ to be our _____. His name is _____.
We can read about his life and teachings in the _____.

LAWS	GOSPELS	JESUS	SAVIOUR
SON	CREATOR	FORGIVES	FATHER
POWERFUL	ETERNAL	SHEPHERD	SHIELD

God speaks to us in the Bible

In the Bible, God chooses different ways to speak to us. Sometimes it is through a story and other times it is in short passages or words of advice. Some of the words comfort us and make us feel good about ourselves, others make us think about the way we treat people and others challenge us to be more generous with our gifts.

Activities

1. Look up the following references and write them out in your own words.

John 14:1	John 14:6	John 14:14
John 15:12	Luke 6:27	Luke 18:29
Matthew 6:19	Matthew 7:1	Matthew 7:12
Matthew 18:21-22	Matthew 22:37	John 14:27

2. Draw 3 faces. Under each face choose a Bible reference from the box above to show how you think others will feel when they read it?

FEELING GOOD   FEELING SAD   FEELING CHALLENGED

3. Look at all the Bible quotations again. Which one will help a person

   (a) who is feeling lost
   (b) to feel good
   (c) to be more generous
   (d) to forgive when he/she has been hurt
   (e) to trust in God

Photocopy Worksheets - The Bible

THE BIBLE
Finding your way around

1. Would you find the following in the Old Testament or New Testament? The first one is done for you.

	O.T	N.T.
(a) God created Heaven and Earth	✓	
(b) The story of Noah, the flood and the Ark	___	___
(c) The Angel Gabriel visits Mary	___	___
(d) The baby Moses is left among the bulrushes	___	___
(e) The book of Psalms	___	___
(f) The Gospel according to Mark	___	___
(g) The story of the baptism of Jesus	___	___

2. In the Old Testament we read of many promises God made to his people. Find one or two of these references and write out the promise with the reference next to it.

Genesis 9:15   Isaiah 54:10   Isaiah 56:1

Photocopy Worksheets - Trust in God

St Joseph trusted in God

Make a 'coat-hanger' poem about St Joseph.

(It's called a coat-hanger poem because you can put words on each side of the letters.)

You could begin like this:

Such a good and gentle man

God **T**rusted him to care for Jesus

J
O
S
E
P
H

In the spaces, draw some things which remind you of St Joseph and his care for Mary and Jesus.

Mary's Song of Praise - The Magnificat

When Mary understood that she was to be the mother of God's Son, she left her home in Nazareth and made a long and difficult journey to visit her cousin Elizabeth. Elizabeth was also going to have a baby.

As soon as Mary arrived, Elizabeth's baby jumped for joy inside her. She said to Mary:

'Blessed are you among women and blessed is the fruit of your womb!' (*Luke 1:42*)

Mary sang a song to God of praise and trust. We call this song the Magnificat. (*Luke 1:46*)

**My soul is filled with joy
As I sing to God my Saviour:
He has looked upon his servant,
He has visited his people**

**And holy is his name
Through all generations!
Everlasting is his mercy
To the people he has chosen,
And holy is his name!**

**I am lowly as a child,
But I know from this day forward
That my name will be remembered,
For all men will call me blessed.**

Mary stayed with Elizabeth for three months. Then she returned home.

ACTIVITIES

1. Imagine you are outside the open window when Mary visits Elizabeth. You overhear these words. Who do you think said them?

    (a) "My baby jumped for joy when you came in!"

    (b) "I am so happy - I will sing a song to praise God."

    (c) "I never thought that the Mother of God's Son would come to visit me!"

    (d) "People will always call me blessed now."

2. Use the words above and some more of your own to make a short play script of the meeting between Elizabeth and Mary.

3. What makes you happy? Draw some gift boxes. Write in each one a gift that God has given you that brings you happiness. Decorate your gift boxes.

4. Mary said in her song that 'all generations' would call her blessed. That means people in every age. When do *we* call Mary blessed?

5. Write a sentence to praise God for all his gifts. In groups, share your sentences, and put them together to make them into a song of praise. Give your song a title.

6. Choose three of these words to describe Mary and say why you chose them.

    CHOSEN   OBEDIENT   HAPPY   BLESSED

    TRUSTING   GENTLE   THOUGHTFUL

7. How can you show your trust in God by trying to be like Mary? Use the words above to help you write some advice to a friend on how to do this. Choose one word to write clearly on a small card or piece of paper, which you can keep near you to remind you to try to be like Mary.

Photocopy Worksheets - Trust in God

Christmas Cards

Look carefully at the Christmas card you have chosen.

What is in the main picture? _____
_____

Which part of the Christmas story is being shown on your card? _____
_____

Why do you think the artist chose this part of the story to put on the card?
_____
_____

Which part of the story would you have chosen? _____
_____
_____

Make a vertical list of the details in the picture. Next to each detail, write why you think the artist put it in.

_____	_____
_____	_____
_____	_____
_____	_____
_____	_____
_____	_____
_____	_____

Choose a small part of your picture and copy it carefully or make a quick sketch of a card you would draw to show the meaning of Christmas.

Photocopy Worksheets - Trust in God

The Flight into Egypt

Joseph always obeyed and trusted God. He became a strong guardian for Mary and for Jesus.

After Jesus was born, Joseph had another dream. In this dream the angel warned him that King Herod wanted to harm Jesus. Joseph trusted God and he believed what the angel told him.

"Rise, take the child and his mother,
and flee to Egypt,
and remain there till I tell you,
for Herod is about to search for the child,
to destroy him." (Matt 2:13)

Joseph had to take Mary and Jesus all the way to Egypt. He had to trust God to look after them and bring them safely home again. The Holy Family lived in Egypt until it was safe for them to return home to Nazareth.

Activities

1. In what ways did Joseph have to trust in God?
   (a) Try to write down two of them.
   (b) Which one do you think was the most difficult?
   Explain why you think this.

2. Many people today have to run away from people who might harm them. They have to leave behind their homes and their friends and go to other countries. We call these people 'refugees', because they are looking for a refuge - a safe place to live.
   (a) Think about the things these people need.
   (b) Think about the things you would want to take with you if you were in that situation.
   (c) Write a prayer asking St Joseph to pray for all refugees.

Photocopy Worksheets - Trust in God

Know how Joseph put his trust in God when the angel appeared to him

Not long after the birth of Jesus, Mary and Joseph had to take the baby and hide in Egypt. Joseph had to trust that God would look after them and Mary had to trust God and Joseph to protect her and Jesus.

Activities

1. Which of these sentences do you think best describes what Mary might have been thinking then?
    - **(a)** "I am very frightened - I'm afraid that some harm might happen to my baby."
    - **(b)** "I am very frightened, but I trust God to keep his promise and he promised that my child would be the Saviour of the world."
    - **(c)** "I don't want to go to Egypt at all. I'm only going because Joseph had a dream."

2. Write out the sentence you chose and say why you chose it.

After a while, King Herod died and the danger passed. Joseph took Mary and Jesus back to Nazareth and Jesus grew up there. Joseph worked very hard as a carpenter and Jesus probably helped him and learned to make things too. We remember St Joseph the Worker on 1st May every year.

3. Design a statue of St Joseph the Worker for your classroom. In your design include some things to show he was a carpenter, that he worked very hard and that he looked after Jesus and Mary.

4. Write an inscription for your statue. Remember, an inscription is just a few words to explain what the statute is.

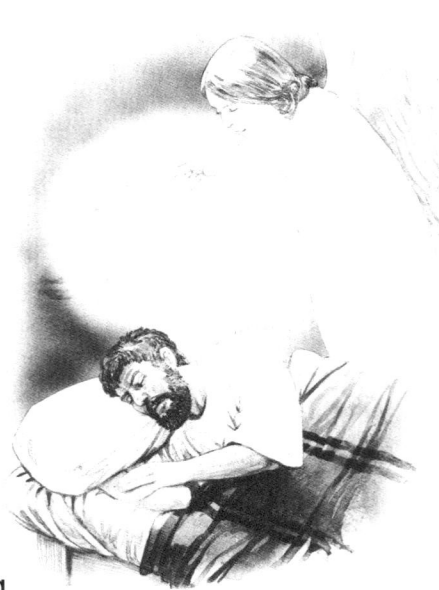

Photocopy Worksheets - Jesus, the Teacher

Jewish Worship of God

Know what Jews believe about the Word of God

Jews believe that the Torah is the Word of God himself, so the scrolls are kept in a special place in the synagogue, called the Ark. There is a curtain in front of the Ark and a light is kept burning near it which is never allowed to go out. This reminds the Jewish people that God is with them in his Word. A candleholder with seven branches called a menorah, stands in front of the Ark.

Match these words with the correct meaning and picture:

Synagogue   Ark   Menorah
   Rabbi   Torah

A.	The building where the Jewish people meet together to pray, to learn the Holy Scriptures and to help each other.
B.	The place in the synagogue where the Word of God is carefully kept.
C.	The first five books (scrolls) of the Old Testament which are especially sacred to the Jewish people.
D.	A candleholder with seven branches which stands in front of the Ark.
E.	Someone who teaches about God, especially in the synagogue.

Photocopy Worksheets - Jesus, the Teacher

Jesus shows us how to live

Helping Others (Do this task with your parents)

1. Choose some people you want to help each day this week in order to try to live as Jesus has taught us.

2. Put the days of the week at the top of each box, some have been done for you.

3. In each box write down the person you want to help and say what you will do.

4. How do you think you will feel at the end of each day if you keep to your plan?

Suggestions:			
mum	dad	grandparents	friend
cousin	aunt	a child refugee	uncle
a sick person	teacher	someone who is lonely	

Everyday	Sunday	Monday	
I will ask Jesus to help me to help other people			

Know the teaching of Jesus

Everyday we will find some opportunity to make the teaching of Jesus come true in our lives. In this way, we will find true happiness, have many friends and give joy to those we meet.

Sometimes the teaching of Jesus is difficult, let us see if we can find ways of making it 'real' in our life and help others to do the same.

1. Choose one piece of advice Jesus gives to us from the list below.
2. Print it onto a sheet of paper, highlight the key words and decorate them.
3. Use bullet points to explain how we can make it 'real' in our lives.

Example:

> **Be different!**
> Why should God reward you if you only love people who love you? That's what everyone else does! (*Luke 6:32*)
>
> When somebody says something hurtful, I will try to be kind.
> When the teacher is cross, I will try to be helpful.

Advice Jesus gives to us

Helping others
In so far as you help others, particularly those who are poor, weak, ill or suffering you are helping Jesus. (*Matthew 25:40*)

The Golden Rule
Treat others, as you would like them to treat you. (*Luke 6:31*)

Don't Find Fault
Do not criticise other people for their tiny faults when all the time you have greater faults yourself. (*Luke 6:41*)

The Great Commandments
Love the Lord your God with all your heart and soul and with all your strength and with all your mind. Love your neighbour as yourself. (*Luke 10:27*)

Forgive
Forgive, not seven times, but seventy-seven times! (*Matthew 18:22*)

Photocopy Worksheets - Jesus, the Teacher

The Great Feast

A man once gave a great feast and invited many people. When the feast was ready, he sent his servant to say to those who had been invited, 'Come to the feast; for everything is ready now.' But they all began to make excuses.

The first said, 'I have bought a field, and I must go out and see it; please have me excused.' And another one said, 'I have bought some new farm animals, and I need to go and look at them; please, have me excused.' And another one said, 'I have just got married, so I can't possibly come!' So the servant went back and told all this to his master. Then the master was very angry and said to his servant, 'Go out quickly into the streets and lanes of the city, and bring in the poor and disabled and blind and hurt.'

The servant did this, then he went back to his master and said, 'Sir, what you commanded has been done, and there is still room.' The master said to the servant, 'Go out to the main roads and make people come in. I want my house to be full. For I tell you, none of those people who were invited shall taste my feast.' (*Luke 14:16-24, adapted*)

Activities

1. (a) What were the excuses the invited guests made?
   (b) What do you think those guests should have done?

2. Imagine you are one of the poor people in the town who were invited afterwards. Write a letter to a friend telling him/her all about it.

3. What do you think is the message that Jesus wanted his followers to understand when he told them this parable?

The Parable of the Sower

People kept coming to Jesus from one town after another; and when a great crowd gathered, Jesus told them this parable:

"Once there was a man who went out to sow corn. As he scattered the seed in the field, some of it fell along the path, where it was stepped on, and the birds ate it up. Some of it fell on rocky ground, and when the plants sprouted, they dried up because the soil had no moisture. Some of the seed fell among thorn bushes, which grew up with the plants and chocked them. And some seed fell in good soil; the plants grew and produced corn, a hundred grains each." (Luke 8:4-8)

GOOD FRIDAY

After Jesus had been arrested and taken away, the others followed at a distance. Peter went into the courtyard of the High Priest's house where Jesus' trial was being held.

Peter tells us what happened:

"It was a chilly night and they'd lit a fire there. I couldn't hear what was going on inside, but I knew they were accusing Jesus of all sorts of things that just weren't true. Suddenly, one of the maids looked straight at me and said to the other servants: "This man was with Jesus too - look!" I turned away, and told her she must have been mistaken. I was scared. What if they'd arrested me too? What if they threw me into prison - or worse? I moved away from the fire.

But then a man approached me. "I'm sure I saw you with him at the Temple this week," he claimed. I glared at him. "Not me!" I said, pulling my cloak around me. Perhaps I should just get out of here, I thought ... Jesus will be able to look after himself. I could go back to Galilee and take up where I left off, fishing in the lake. Ah, Galilee! I missed my home and my family and... "He's a Galilean!" someone called out to the others. "Just listen to his accent!" "Leave me alone", I shouted. "I have no idea what you're talking about!"

Photocopy Worksheets - Jesus, the Saviour

> At that moment, I heard the cock crow and remembered what Jesus had said to me over supper. "Before the cock crows, Peter," he'd told me, "You'll have said three times that you don't know me." I'd insisted that he was wrong - that I'd never deny him. But he'd been right, hadn't he? When challenged, I'd said I hadn't known him. I felt really ashamed of myself and ran out of the courtyard, tears streaming down my face. How could he ever forgive me? I didn't deserve to be called his friend!"
> (*See Luke 22:54-62*)

Activities

1. Sometimes we have an 'argument' inside our minds. Our conscience might say, "You shouldn't have done that". We might say, "I couldn't help it." Write one speech bubble for Peter's conscience and one for his reply.

2. If you had met Peter after he heard the cock crow

    (a) What would you have said to him?

    (b) How would you have tried to help him?

    (c) What do you think Jesus would say to him?

Photocopy Worksheets - Jesus, the Saviour

Holy Week: What happened when?

Cut up the pieces of paper and re-arrange them in the correct order to tell the story of what happened in Holy Week.

If you wish, you can fill in parts of the story that are missing.

Mary Magdalene found the stone rolled away from the tomb.

Jesus celebrated the Passover meal with the disciples.

Jesus was crucified on a cross.

Jesus had risen from the dead.

Judas showed the guards where Jesus was.

Jesus had to carry his cross to Calvary.

Peter claimed he had never known Jesus.

Jesus found Peter, James and John fast asleep.

Photocopy Worksheets - Jesus, the Saviour

Holy Week

DAY	WHAT HAPPENED?	Where can I find this in the Bible?
SUNDAY	Jesus rides into Jerusalem on a donkey	Mark 19:28-40
MONDAY		
TUESDAY		
WEDNESDAY		
THURSDAY		
FRIDAY		
SATURDAY		
SUNDAY		

Photocopy Worksheets - Jesus, the Saviour

Easter Liturgy

Teacher: Today, let us celebrate our belief that Jesus rose from the dead, that he is alive and he is with us.

Jesus, Risen from the Dead

Easter Sunday

A reading from the Gospel of Luke

On the first day of the week, at the first sign of dawn, they (the women) went to the tomb with the spices they had prepared. They found that the stone had been rolled away from the tomb, but on entering discovered that the body of the Lord Jesus was not there. As they stood there not knowing what to think, two men in brilliant clothes suddenly appeared at their side. Terrified, the women lowered their eyes. But the two men said to them, 'Why look among the dead for someone who is alive? He is not here; he is risen. Remember what he told you when he was still in Galilee: that the Son of Man had to be handed over into the power of sinful men and be crucified, and rise again on the third day.' And they remembered his words. *(Luke 24:1-8)*

Group 1 Jesus, you are risen from the dead.
Response Jesus, we believe it.

Group 2 Jesus, you promised to be with us always.
Response Jesus, we believe it.

Group 3 Jesus, you are present in the Blessed Sacrament.
Response Jesus, we believe it.

Group 4 Jesus, you have promised us eternal life.
Response Jesus, we believe it.

Group 5 Jesus, you have promised to send us the Holy Spirit.
Response Jesus, we believe it.

Teacher: Jesus, today, we ask you to increase our faith, hope and love in you.

[Finish with Easter Song or hymn]

Photocopy Worksheets - Mission of the Church

Prayers to the Holy Spirit

1. Use these **Prayers** to help you to plan a liturgy to the **Holy Spirit**.

> Holy Spirit, I want to know you and love you and serve you.
> Come into my mind and help me understand.
> Come into my heart and help me to love you.
> Come into my soul and make me strong to do your work.
> Amen.

The following can be used as a prayer or sung to the tune of 'Give me peace, Oh Lord, I pray' (HON 160)

Holy Spirit, friend of mine,
Stand beside me all the time,
Help me know what I should do,
Teach me through the day.

Holy Spirit, friend of mine,
Live inside me all the time,
Help me know how I can pray,
Fill me through the day.

Holy Spirit, friend of mine,
Walk before me all the time,
Help me know how I can serve,
Guide me through the day.

2. With a partner, learn this prayer to the Holy Spirit. You can each take one part to learn, so that the whole class will be able to offer the prayer in two groups.

A. Come, Holy Spirit, fill the hearts of your faithful.
B. **And kindle in them the fire of your love.**

A. Send forth your spirit, Lord, and they shall be created.
B. **And you shall renew the face of the earth.**

Photocopy Worksheets - Mission of the Church

Peter and Paul

Peter used to be Simon and Paul used to be Saul. But more than their names changed when they began to do God's work. Look at the words in the box and write them in the best places on the diagram.

frightened	confident	angry	worried
thoughtless	cruel	calm	strong
embarrassed	unsure	certain	anxious
hardworking	sorry	brave	

BEFORE

Simon	Saul

AFTER

Peter	Paul

Use the words you have put in one section to draw a picture or write a short description of either Peter or Paul.

Photocopy Worksheets - Mission of the Church

What can we do to prepare for our mission?

Take steps

Help...

Forgive others...

Study...

Tasks

1. Under each step write down all the things you can do to make you a better person.
2. Choose three that you think are the most important and explain why.
3. What steps did St Paul have to take before he became a missionary?

Photocopy Worksheets - Belonging to the Church

Our Parish Church Project

The aim of this project is to train you to act as a guide for your Parish Church. It may happen that people of other faiths will request a guided tour. Also, it will give you the opportunity to introduce other pupils in your class to your church.

Plan

- You could work in Parish Groups.

- You are asked to prepare a talk about your Church and all the different things in it:
  - name of Church, altar, tabernacle, lectern, priest's chair, baptistery, crucifix, statues and stained glass windows.

- You will need to prepare visual aids to help you with your talk - you may use drawings, sketches, photos or a video.

- You will need to appoint a group leader who will make sure that everybody in the group has an important task to do. Set deadlines for these tasks to be done.

- Every member of the group will need to visit the Parish Church in order to see all the things he/she has to speak or write about.

- If you need more information, you may wish to speak to one of the priests in the Parish. Please be sure to telephone first to make an appointment to see him.

Assessment of Project
- Discuss with your teacher how marks will be awarded.
- Extra marks will be given for imaginative presentation, including use of computer, camera, video camera etc.

Our Parish Church

Here are some questions you need to be able to answer.

Why is there an altar?
It is a table on which the bread and wine are changed into the body and blood of Jesus during Mass. It is the place where the sacrifice of Jesus is made present for us.

Why is there a lectern?
A lectern is a sign of the importance we give to the Bible: the Word of God.

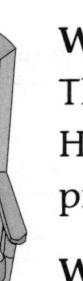

Why does the priest have a special chair?
The priest represents Jesus, so he has an important seat. He sits down to listen to the readings from the Bible and to pray silently.

Why is there a tabernacle?
After Mass the consecrated Hosts, which we call the Blessed Sacrament, are kept in the tabernacle. Many people wish to pray privately in front of the Blessed Sacrament in our churches.

Why is there a crucifix?
The crucifix reminds us of the death of Jesus on the cross.

Why do people genuflect when they go into church?
They genuflect out of respect for the presence of Jesus in the Blessed Sacrament in the tabernacle.

Why are there Stations of the Cross around the walls of the church?
Many people go around the Stations of the Cross particularly during Lent. They reflect on what Jesus has suffered for us and pray to him.

Levels of Achievement

ASSESSMENT & LEVELS OF ACHIEVEMENT

Introduction
Good assessment should have variety, flexibility and be based on the professional judgement of teachers. Schools will wish to develop a range of assessment tasks, such as spoken, creative or written work. Assessment should be on going, not added on.

Formative assessment
Formative assessment goes on all the time. It includes oral responses, self-evaluation, target setting, marking and Records of Achievement. It is formative because it points out what is good and how it could be improved.

Summative assessment
This summarises and reports on what has been learnt. It is helpful to create 'contexts' when setting tasks. One way of doing it is to create an imaginary problem. For example, Jane had to go into hospital and has been away from school for three weeks. During that time she missed out on what happens in Holy Week. Can you tell her all that she needs to know using the following headings?

The Parable of the Sower: Jesus describes all of us at different times in our lives. What are we like when we are the seeds that fall;
(a) among thorns _____
(b) on good soil _____
(c) on rocky places _____
I need help to understand why _____
What I enjoy doing most in the lessons is ___

Holy Week
On Palm Sunday _____
On Holy Thursday _____
On Good Friday _____
On Easter Sunday _____
The most important thing to remember is __
_____ because _____

Self evaluation
The following prompts may help pupils to assess their own learning.

Mission of the Church

I enjoyed _____ because _____

I found _____ difficult, because _____

I can now tell others about _____

I think my best piece of work was _____

I can improve by _____

Levels of Achievement

The following is guidance for teachers to help them map pupils' progress. Teachers may feel that they also need to give pupils feedback in a different form in order to motivate and give them a sense of achievement.

The Level Descriptors are based on National Expectations in Religious Education produced by the Qualifications and Curriculum Authority (QCA). The QCA descriptors have been modified so that they apply specifically to Catholic religious education content.

The overview on page 82 provides examples of how a pupil might attain a particular level. The exemplar assessment tasks based on each module or unit of work are intended as guidance for the teacher.

Attainment Target 1 (AT1) = Learning **ABOUT** the Catholic Faith

Attainment Target 2 (AT2) = Learning **FROM** the Catholic Faith

OVERVIEW of GRID
A B C = AT1
D E F = AT2

Range of levels within which the majority of pupils are expected to work	Expected attainment for the majority of pupils at the end of the key stage
Key Stage 1 L1 - 3	At the age of 7 L2
Key Stage 2 L2 - 5	At the age of 11 L4

Levels of Achievement

Level	A Beliefs & teachings (what people believe)	B Practices & lifestyles (what people do)	C Expression & language (how people express themselves)	D Identity & experience (making sense of who we are)	E Meaning & purpose (making sense of life)	F Values & commitments (making sense of right & wrong)
1	Tell a story	Recognise what we are doing when e.g. we pray	Recognise the meaning of some words: e.g. Holy Communion; Jesus, our Saviour	Be able to say why it is important to learn about e.g. Jesus, forgiveness		Know the difference between a good action and a bad one
2	Indicate what is important about it	What are some of the things Christians do? Do other religions do these things?	Suggest their meaning	Respond sensitively to the feelings of others	Be aware that some questions are difficult to answer, e.g. Who is God?	Be sensitive to what people believe about matters of right & wrong
3	Describe a belief or teaching and say why it is important	What are some of the big events Christians celebrate? For example: Holy Week	Explain the use of some religious language: e.g. Jesus died to take away our sins; to give us eternal life in heaven		Compare their own & other people's ideas about questions that are difficult to answer e.g. Why did Jesus die on the cross?	Make links between matters of right and wrong & their own behaviour
4		Show some understanding of what Catholics/Christians believe and how this should affect the way they live	Show how religious ideas & beliefs can be expressed in a variety of forms, giving meanings for some parables/stories /psalms	Ask questions about key figures & suggest answers from own and other's experience	Ask questions about significant experiences of key figures and suggest answers, e.g. What does the resurrection of Jesus mean for us?	Ask questions on matters of right & wrong; suggest answers that show understanding of moral & religious issues
5	Explain how some beliefs & teachings can make a difference to peoples' lives	Explain how the teaching of Jesus could make a difference to the lives of others: e.g. to love one another & to love your enemies (Jn 15:12 & Matt 5:44)		Make informed responses to questions of identity & experience in light of learning	Make informed responses to questions of meaning in light of learning, e.g. What is the message of some of the parables for us?	Make informed responses to moral issues in the light of learning, e.g. stealing, telling lies etc.

Assessment Tasks

MODULE 1: THE BIBLE

ASSESSMENT TASKS

1. Imagine that Fernando, a new pupil, has arrived. You have been studying the Bible for two weeks so your teacher asks you to explain to him what the Bible is about. What would you tell him? [AT1 L1]

2. Can you tell Fernando about one story you know from the Bible and explain why the story is important? [AT1 L2]

3. The Bible tells us that God asked Abraham to leave his home and start out on a journey. He would only discover what it was all about as he went along.

   (a) How do you think Sarah, his wife, felt when he told her that they would be leaving to go on a long journey?
   (b) What would you miss most if you had to move house and leave almost everything behind? [AT2 L3]

4. Jonah was a prophet who did not want to obey God.

   (a) What lessons did he have to learn?
   (b) How did God teach Jonah these lessons? [AT1 L2]
   (c) What can we learn from the story of Jonah? [AT2 L3]

5. Imagine you have the chance to talk to Jonah.

   (a) What questions would you ask him?
   (b) What do you think he would tell you? [AT2 L4]

MODULE 2: TRUST IN GOD

ASSESSMENT TASKS

1. Tell the story of the promise God made to Mary [AT1 L1]
   and explain why it was very important [AT1 L2]

2. In the story of Zechariah we are told that he found it difficult to believe in the promise that the angel made to him. Because of this, he could not speak for a long time. Pretend you are Zechariah and write down what he might have written for his family when he came home from the temple. [AT2 L2]

3. Look at this list of things Mary had to trust God to do when she said 'yes' to him. Mary had to trust God:

   - to make Joseph understand that her baby was the Son of God;
   - to let the baby be born safely in the place God chose;
   - to protect her and the baby from all danger.

   (a) Choose one of these and explain why Mary might have been anxious. You could begin like this: "Mary might have been worried that..."
   (b) Describe a time when you have been worried but, like Mary, you trusted in God. [AT2 L2-3]

4. Imagine you meet Mary and Joseph with the baby Jesus on their way into Egypt. You get talking to them and want to find out why they are making such a long journey with a tiny baby.

   (a) What questions would you ask them?
   (b) Write down the answers you think they would give you. [AT2 L4]

5. Many people today have to run away from people who might harm them. They have to leave behind their homes and their friends and go to other countries. We call these people 'refugees', because they are looking for a refuge - a safe place to live.

   (a) Do you know of any people who had to leave their country?
   (b) Do you think we should help these people? Why? [AT2 L3-4]

MODULE 3: JESUS, THE TEACHER

ASSESSMENT TASKS

1. Imagine you were in the Temple when Mary and Joseph arrived with the baby Jesus, can you describe what you saw and heard? [AT1 L1]

2. Jesus came to show us the way to live.

    (a) Write down two things that he has asked us to do. [AT1 L2]
    (b) Why is it important that we follow the teaching of Jesus? [AT1 L3]

3. Read the parable of 'The Unforgiving Servant' (Matt 18:23-25)

    (a) Who do you think is most like God in this parable?
    (b) What was the lesson that Jesus wanted the people to understand from this parable?
    (c) What do you think is the lesson in this parable for us today? [AT2 L3-4]

4. You have been studying the parable of 'The Sower' - now make notes to help you remember it.

    (a) Draw three places where the seed fell and beside each drawing write an explanation of what happened to the seed and why it happened. [AT1 L4]

5. Imagine you were present when Jesus told the parable of 'The Sower'.

    (a) What questions would you want to ask him in order to fully understand what it means?
    (b) What do you think he would say in reply? [AT2 L4-5]

Assessment Tasks

MODULE 4: JESUS, THE SAVIOUR

ASSESSMENT TASKS

1. A friend of yours, who is not a Christian, asked you why Good Friday is a very important day. Can you tell him what happened to Jesus on Good Friday? [AT1 L1]

2. Jesus "is truly God and, as a man, truly human". Why do you think some people might find this difficult to understand? [AT2 L2-3]

3. Imagine you are a journalist sent by the BBC to Jerusalem to report on what happened on Holy Thursday. You meet John, the disciple, and ask him what happened at the Last Supper.

   (a) Write down the questions you would want to ask him.
   (b) Now write down the answers you think he would give you. [AT2 L4]

4. On Good Friday, after Jesus had been taken away by the guards, Peter was scared in case they would also arrest him. He was asked if he was a follower of Jesus and he said he did not even know him.

   If you had met Peter after he heard the cock crow;
   (a) what would you have said to him?
   (b) how would you have tried to help him?
   (c) what do you think Jesus would say to him when he met him again? [AT2 L5]

5. On Easter Sunday, we celebrate the resurrection of Jesus from the dead. Why is this a very important event for all people? [AT1 L3]

MODULE 5: MISSION OF THE CHURCH

ASSESSMENT TASKS

1. The pupils in Year 1 have heard that Jesus rose from the dead. Write a story to tell them of how he was seen alive again by other people. [AT1 L1]

2. Why do you think it is very important for all of us to know the story of the resurrection of Jesus from the dead? [AT1 L2]

3. Imagine you have to explain who Jesus is to someone who has never heard of him. Make an information leaflet about Jesus. Put in the most important things about him. [AT1 L3]

4. After the resurrection, Jesus appeared to the disciples on the beach - they had been out fishing.
   Read the story in John 21:1-11.
   (a) What do you think Jesus wanted to say to his disciples while they were having breakfast?
   (b) What would you have wanted to say to Jesus if you had been one of the disciples?
   (c) What answers do you think he would have given to your questions? [AT2 L4]

5. You have been studying the Mission of the Church. Think about how you can be part of it.
   (a) Who can you tell about Jesus?
   (b) What can you tell them?
   (c) What can you do to show love for others?
   (d) How can you live as Jesus asks?
   (e) Can you give an example of how Jesus has helped you or someone else? [AT1 L4]

Assessment Tasks

MODULE 6: BELONGING TO THE CHURCH

ASSESSMENT TASKS

1. Imagine some inspectors are visiting the school. They know it is a Catholic school and they want to find out from the pupils what Catholics believe. In order to help them, write down;

    (a) what you think Catholics believe about Jesus;
    (b) what it means to belong to the community of the Church.   [AT1 L3]

2. Imagine one of the inspectors asked you what a person had to do in order to become a member of the Church. What would you reply?   [AT1 L2]

3. Describe one of the great feasts that the Church celebrates and say why it is important.   [AT1 L3]

4. Every school has to have rules.

    (a) What do you think are some of the most important rules for a Catholic school?
    (b) What should people notice most of all about the behaviour of pupils in the school?   [AT2 L3]

5. Imagine your parish church was burnt down during the night. What do you think the newspapers would be able to say about the people who belonged to it?
   How do you think it might affect you and your family?   [AT2 L4]

Marking Assessment Tasks

GUIDANCE ON LEVELS OF ACHIEVEMENT ASSESSMENT

The Bible

1. AT1 L1   A story about God and his people. It has many stories.
2. AT1 L2   Can briefly outline a story and say something about its importance.
3. AT2 L3   (a) Is able to empathise with Sarah - felt sad, upset, did not understand.
   (b) Shows some understanding of what it would involve.
4. AT1 L2   (a) Jonah had to learn to obey and to trust God.
   (b) God had to teach Jonah by making him aware that he could not escape from God - accept pupil's description of storm and Jonah in the whale - but in the end God rescued Jonah.
   AT2 L3   (c) To listen to the voice of God within us and do what we think God is asking of us. Or, because God loves us he will correct us if we do wrong.
5. AT2 L4   Accept any questions/replies, which show some understanding of what happened in the story.

Trust in God

1. AT1 L1   Is able to briefly outline the story of the Annunciation.
   AT1 L2   It is important because Mary was going to be the mother of God.
2. AT2 L2   Accept any attempt to explain what happened in the temple.
3. AT2 L2-3   (a) Accept any answer that shows understanding of Mary's anxiety.
   (b) Is able to describe an experience of anxiety and trust in God.
4. AT2 L4   Is able to ask questions/suggest answers that focus on the reasons for the long journey with a tiny baby.
5. AT2 L3-4   Shows some understanding of the problems facing refugees and how as Christians we should try to help them - love of neighbour.

Jesus, the Teacher

1. AT1 L1   Can briefly describe what happened.
2. AT1 L2   (a) Love God and our neighbour or love our enemies, pray for those who persecute us.
   AT1 L3   (b) Because if we want to be a true follower of Jesus we have to accept his teaching.
3. AT2 L3-4   (a) The king.
   (b) Since Jesus is always ready to forgive us, if we ask him, when we do something wrong, so we should be ready to forgive others.
   (c) This is very similar to (b) - it just makes it personal.
4. AT1 L4   Good soil - people who hear the message and live by it.
   Rocky places - give up when trouble comes.
   Thorns - those who do not understand, because other things have stopped them.
   Path - worried by other things and ignore it. (Any three of the above).
5. AT2 L4-5   Able to ask questions about puzzling aspects of life as described in the parable and can make some responses in the light of their learning.

Marking Assessment Tasks

Jesus, the Saviour

1.	AT1 L1	He died on a cross, or he was put to death.
2.	AT2 L2	An awareness that some questions that cause us to wonder are difficult to answer.
	AT2 L3	Able to express an opinion about why people might find this a difficult question.
3.	AT2 L4	Able to ask significant questions about the Last Supper and suggest appropriate answers.
4.	AT2 L5	Able to make informed comments to Peter and respond in the light of learning as to how Jesus treated Peter after betrayal.
5.	AT1 L3	The resurrection of Jesus proves that death is not the end and that if we believe and trust in him, we will be able to have true happiness now and to live forever with him in heaven.

Mission of the Church

1.	AT1 L1	A brief outline of any of the resurrection appearances.
2.	AT1 L2	It is important for us to know about the resurrection - because this shows us that death is not the end, God has power over death.
3.	AT1 L3	His birth, something on his teaching and death & resurrection.
4.	AT2 L4	Can suggest conversation in light of learning; ask questions and make appropriate responses.
5.	AT1 L4	Can make appropriate responses to questions in the light of learning.

Belonging to the Church

1.	AT1 L3	(a) Jesus is the Son of God, born in a stable that he died on the cross and rose again from the dead. (b) We have to be baptised, to follow the teaching of Jesus and (if possible) to go to Mass on Sundays.
2.	AT1 L2	To receive the Sacrament of Baptism.
3.	AT1 L3	Christmas - the birth of Jesus; Jesus has come down on earth to share our life so that we can share his, or, Easter - the resurrection of Jesus from the dead; The resurrection of Jesus proves that death is not the end and that if we believe and trust in him, we will be able to have true happiness now and to live forever with him in heaven.
4.	AT2 L3	(a) An awareness of the commandment to love God and our neighbour as ourselves/ be ready to forgive. (b) A happy community where everybody helps each other.
5.	AT2 L4	Can make an informed response - the real 'church' is the people, they can find another place to worship - that's what is most important. People might find ways of praying together and having Mass in their own homes and inviting others.

Appendix: "Praying Twice"

Some songs to accompany the units of Book 4, with suggestions and comments.

Introduction

"The one who sings, prays twice" (*St Augustine of Hippo*). This saying from the early Christian community reminds us of the central place that sacred song has always had in the Church. Singing is an activity which makes physical and emotional demands on us - it requires a level of involvement by us as whole people, as we breathe, use our muscles, listen to ourselves and each other, and articulate and understand words.

In working with children (and adults) it can be that singing multiplies prayer in other ways. Songs help us remember and carry around with us our prayers, bits of scripture, ideas and feelings. At their best sacred songs are like mobile and accessible bits of theology which can be sung, prayed, hummed and whistled on buses, in the kitchen, at bedtime...

The songs suggested below have been drawn up with the contents of each unit especially in mind, as well as the ages of the children who are most likely to be using the material. Not all the words and sentiments are immediately accessible to children; they are not meant to be! Part of our education in prayer, and theology (thought about faith) is to work with the slightly difficult, the not immediately obvious, led and helped by those accompanying us - teachers and fellow learners. For this reason, a number of the songs have a line or two suggesting how they might be spoken of in relation to the work done in the unit. Here these connections are expressed in an adult form for teachers to think about; when we, as teachers, have "entered the song" we can truly communicate it as prayer and theology for our children.

Theology, double prayer, and fun and moving too!

There is, in our progress in the faith, a spiral movement as we revisit familiar themes with new insights, new maturity and new experiences. Many of the songs from Book 3 may be appropriate for use in relation to the Book 4 units also; indeed, part of the importance of good sacred song is becoming familiar with words through music, so allowing them to grow deeper into our prayer and understanding.

In what follows further suggestions are made, some of which are chosen particularly as they are more challenging to the children as they grow older. As they begin to think more about their faith, children can be invited to make explicit connections between the songs they like singing and passages from scripture, and the parts of the Mass. Wherever possible these connections have been drawn out in the short notes accompanying these suggested songs.

References have been made to "Hymns Old and New" except where a song does not appear in that book; but teachers should be aware that many of the more well-known songs can be found in most of the more commonly used hymnals. Abbreviations and references are as follows:

References are made to: Hymns Old and New (with Supplement) Kevin Mayhew 1989. Abbrev. HON
Laudate Decani Music 1999. Abbrev. L
The Source. Compiled Graham Kendrick. Kevin Mayhew 1998. Abbrev. S
Music for the Mass vol 1 Geoffrey Chapman 1987. Abbrev. MM

Praying Twice

The Bible

O the word of my Lord (HON 431)
The "word" here is addressed to the deep places of our being. This provides an opportunity to reflect on what the 'wisdom' gained from Scripture might be: not just cleverness, or knowing things, but something deeper.

There are many good contemporary settings of psalms, which might appeal to children of this age. I would suggest particularly:
The Lord's my Shepherd (HON 768)
On Eagle's Wings (HON 783)
Blest be the Lord (HON 678)
The Lord hears the cry of the poor (HON 765)

These Psalm settings, and others, can be used to introduce the children to the psalms:
My soul proclaims (HON 68)
My soul is filled with joy (HON 365)

Mary herself is one typified by trusting in God's word, as she pondered on it in the Hebrew scriptures ("Old Testament"):

We often think of prayer, especially with our children, in terms of asking God to hear us; and there is a place for this. It is also important that we learn to open our ears and hearts to him, and so learn to pray more deeply that we will hear Him, especially in his Word. A number of the above songs reflect this. See also:
Spirit of the living God (HON 501)
Be still and know (HON 58)

Trust in God

Trust in the Lord is something that all of us need to both celebrate and pray for.
Walk with me, O my Lord (HON 582)
A simple song asking for a greater trust. Note the reference to the calming of the stormy sea in vs. 3, linking with the work done in the unit.
Be still, and know I am with you (HON 57)
Easy to sing, this song draws us to reflect that Jesus has given us his word that he will always be with us. This is a word to be trusted.
Father, I place into your hands (HON 133)
At the heart of trust in God is the ability simply to let go of our worries and troubles, let the Lord take care of them. Simple, but not easy!
Do not worry (HON 123)
A cheerful celebration of Jesus' assurance to us all that we will be looked after.
Do not be afraid (HON 122)
"Do not be afraid" appears frequently in the Bible (over 300 times) and is the common greeting from God to men and women: see the greeting of the angel to both Zechariah and Mary. In this song the promise of God to his prophet Isaiah (cf. Is 43) is reflected on, quietly and movingly.

It should be made clear that the coming of Jesus not only fulfils a promise to Mary, but is the fulfilment of God's promise to his People Israel, made, in different ways, to Abraham, Moses, and, especially David. The following songs reflect something of this:
Lord, Emmanuel, Come (L 82)
"Emmanuel", God-with-us, is God's response to the longing of all creation, and all history, and his response to the restlessness of our own hearts.

Praying Twice

O come, O come (HON 384)
A central part of the Advent tradition of the Christian Church, this ancient hymn can be thoughtfully used with children, although it is not without challenges! In this context, a selection of verses may be used, and attention drawn to the names given to Jesus: "Emmanuel"; "Rod of Jesse"; "Key of David". Throughout reference is made to the history of Israel, permeated, as it is, by the trust that the Messiah will come.

Long ago, prophets knew (L 116)
The words - to this familiar tune - reflect both the history of Israel, the Christmas story, and also the trust that Christ will come to us today if we welcome him into our hearts.

Be bold, be strong (S 38)
To celebrate St Joseph, as someone who "walked in faith".

God is good (S 124)

Though the mountains may fall (HON 569)

Jesus, the Teacher

To help in this unit we can look at songs that illustrate some of the themes which come out of reflecting on Jesus' teaching. In what follows, songs are arranged under headings which reflect the points arising from the unit. Wherever possible songs have been chosen that are based on Jesus' own words as we have them in the Gospels.

General: Jesus as Teacher
God's Spirit is in my heart (HON 183)
Jesus the Lord said (L 746)
The light of Christ (HON 529)
Christ illuminates what was dark, and brings new life by his teaching. In particular, he teaches repentance and freedom from sin (vs. 3)

The Kingdom
Seek ye first (HON 473)
It is a good exercise to see where these words come in Jesus' own teaching. Children can be led into discussing what "seeking the Kingdom" (and God's "righteousness"!) might mean, getting clues from the scriptural text.

Blest are you (HON 68)
Again, based on Jesus' own words, this is a simple song, which can be repeated and reflected on, helping development of ideas about God's Kingdom, or reign.

Rejoice! Rejoice! (L 818)
An inspiring contemporary song, which speaks to us of the closeness of the Kingdom, and the way in which we are called to respond in building up the Kingdom on earth.

Repentance and Forgiveness
The "praying Twice" section for Book 3, unit 3.3 has some suggestions for songs reflecting on forgiveness and change, which are appropriate here as well. In addition the following might usefully be added. What is important in all of them is the ability they have to deepen our sense of repentance beyond just saying, or even being, sorry; rather repentance is about a change of heart, a turning point.

Return to God (L 193)

Grant to us, O lord (HON 699)
Best sung simply, and unaccompanied. Note, again, the scripture which is the song's source.

O lord, all the world belongs to you (L 847)
Very bright, and bouncy, this song picks up how Jesus changes everything, turning things upside down, and gives us a new mission and ethical direction.

Praying Twice

Care for the Poor

Christ is our King (HON 84)

Bright, and easy to pick up, this song sums up Christ's mission on earth.

Christ be our light (L 883)

Very popular with and well-sung by children, this song combines a joyful sense of Christ's presence with us (refrain) with a strong and uncompromising sense of mission.

Servant song (L 924)

It may also be worth referring pupils back to the Magnificat, and its strong sense of God's justice, and His favour for the poor and oppressed.

Love one another

This is my will (HON 557)

A simple and immediate musical reflection on the words of Jesus as we have them in John's Gospel. Also along these lines:

A new commandment (HON 39)

Let there be love (HON 726)

One of those simple, rousing songs, to which verses can be added easily.

Ubi Caritas (HON 772)

This simple Taize chant can be repeated as a meditation in response to scripture. It offers an opportunity to introduce children to the use of Latin, which can open up for us all sorts of questions about what it means to "understand" when we pray and worship. This is a very ancient part of the Holy Thursday liturgy, related to the washing of the feet, and this might be borne in mind, also. It is, after all, at the Last Supper, that we see most clearly what Christian love is about; this is especially clear in John's Gospel.

Bind us together (HON 62)

God is love (HON 178)

Something of an old favourite, this hymn makes clear the relationship between our call to love, and God's own love and his nature as love.

Jesus, the Saviour

This unit covers some very profound, and theologically complex material. The Incarnation and the Atonement are central theological themes from earliest time. There is a danger that, as teachers of children, we either over-simplify or try to say too much. Often the poetry of song - even when couched in difficult language - can bring us to a deeper understanding, as well as a strong sense of mystery. It is in this spirit that the following are suggested.

All heaven declares (L 760)

An Easter song, it has its roots firmly in the incarnation and passion.

At the name of Jesus (HON 50)

I would suggest the second tune for children, which is very lively. This is a theologically ambitious song, spanning creation, incarnation, passion and resurrection in its seven verses, but centring always on the person of Jesus. It is best taken as the telling of the story of our redemption, and might be talked through a bit at a time, using different verses to illustrate different parts of the module of work.

Majesty! (HON 735)

A real favourite with children! Its apparent simplicity shouldn't prevent our seeing that what is being spoken of here is the mysterious conviction that it is the same Jesus who was crucified, who is now raised, and sits with the Father in heaven, King of all.

Lord Jesus Christ (HON 326)

A strong sense of Christ's real presence with us here, and the telling of the story of his passion, death and resurrection as "Mary's son" and "Son of God".

Praying Twice

In illustrating the events of Holy Week explored in this unit, it is good when songs can be used that are shared by the parish community(-ies) of which the children are a part.

Come to Jerusalem (L231)
This has the added advantage of an Israeli tune, which links up with the module's work on the Jewishness of Jesus and his ministry.

Jesu, Jesu (L 241)
A simple musical meditation on the washing of the feet at the last supper, and its meaning for us as disciples.

Ubi caritas (HON 772)
A traditional part of the Holy Thursday Liturgy, this simple repetitive chant makes clear that the Last Supper expressed Christ's love for his friends, and the call that we all have to love.

This is my body (HON 556)

Stay with me (HON 760)
A simple Taize chant to aid reflection on the Garden of Gethsemane.

Jesus, remember me (HON 717)
Again, a simple chant from Taize, based on the words of the thief crucified with Jesus.

He is risen, tell the story (HON 207)

Sing to the mountains (HON 495)

Mission of the Church

I will be with you (HON 263)
This song reflects both the post-resurrection appearances of Jesus to his disciples, and the mission that he set before them. It makes clear that this mission is set before us too, as is Jesus' promise to be with us always.

We'll walk the land (S 551)
A wonderfully rousing contemporary song of mission and pilgrimage.

All over the world (HON 26)
This emphatically makes the link between the work of the Spirit and the renewal of the world through Christian mission and the activity of the Holy Spirit in it.

This is the Day (HON 560)
A song of Resurrection and Pentecost, which is simple to sing and joyful. It can be used to pose the question (no answers really needed!) about the present reality of Pentecost and Easter - these things are the source of our joy and mission in the here and now.

The Spirit lives to set us free (HON 547)
This well-known, and easily sung song carries in it a strong sense of mission, relating it to the passion and resurrection, and the sending of the Spirit. The "walk in the light" refrain can, perhaps, be too easily glossed over; but its message of keeping moving, pilgrimage and being sent out shouldn't be missed.

Spirit of the Living God (HON 501)
The module seeks to make clear how it is the sending of the Holy Spirit that makes it possible for the disciples to carry on Jesus' mission after he has ascended into heaven. This song is a simple prayer asking for that same Spirit to come to us now - to melt us, and mould us, and *use* us for the building up of the Kingdom.

If God is for us (HON 231)
This stirring and lovely song not only clearly conveys the strength of the apostolic mission in Christ, but it also draws on the writings of St Paul - a central person to this unit. Again, what is clear is that Christ is with us, always, and that we have freedom in his Spirit.

Praying Twice

Belonging to the Church

A new commandment (HON 39)
Above all it is Christ's commandment to love one another (even when that means people we might normally avoid!) which makes us a Christian community.

One bread, one Body (HON 744)
A wonderful, scripturally based contemporary hymn this makes clear the nature of our community as focussed on the Eucharistic table. It also draws our attention to the language of the Body - important Biblical language for understanding belonging to the Church, which might be gently introduced at this stage.

Come and praise Him (HON 91)
At our baptism we are anointed, one in Christ, priests, prophets and kings. This song might effectively be used to illustrate meditation on 1 Peter 2:9 - "a people set apart to sing God's praises".

Into the family of God (L 405)
A cheerful celebration for baptism, emphasising the nature of the baptised community as the family of God.

I believe in Jesus (S 195)
A song with a strong, attractive contemporary feel, which can be used to illustrate the importance of what Christians believe - especially about the work of Jesus. This conviction, as expressed here and in scripture, is not just a belief about what has happened, but also a 'sureness' about the living reality of Jesus' power among us in the Spirit.

Welcome all ye noble saints (HON 595)
A good gathering song for a service of prayer, or the Eucharist, this hymn highlights how the communion of saints and prophets is one with us as we gather to worship.

O when the saints (HON 437)
Bound to raise a smile, this very well-known song can still spring us into more serious reflection on what it means to be called to join the saints in heaven. It is actually rather challenging to us to realise how these words refer us to the "Last Things", and call us, as God's saints, to look beyond the here and now to the things of heaven.

For all the saints who showed your love (L 387)
A gentle, familiar tune serves well this reflection on the "ordinary" saints of the church - the holy men and women with whom we have communion in Christ, even though we have never known them.

It might also be useful to recall that, at the singing of the "holy, holy" in the Mass we particularly remember that we are one with "all the angels and saints". These are, in fact, the words of the song which, St John tells us, is sung in heaven - Revelation 4:8.